D0646884

The COAST
of British Columbia

The COAST
of British Columbia

Photography by Bob Herger
Text by Rosemary Neering

Alaska Northwest Books
Anchorage • Seattle

Copyright © 1990 by Bob Herger and
    Rosemary Neering

All rights reserved. No part of this
publication may be reproduced or
transmitted in any form or by any
means, electronic or mechanical, including photocopying, recording, or
by any information storage and re-
trieval system, without written per-
mission of Alaska Northwest Books™.

Published in Canada by Whitecap
    Books Limited
Edited by Brian Scrivener
Photographs by Bob Herger
Additional photography by Steve
    Short, p. 56, 57; Dale Sanders, p. 72,
    73
Cover design and interior design by
    Brad Nickason and Peter Tom
Map by Heather Rankin
Typeset at Vancouver Desktop
    Publishing Centre Ltd.
Separations by Camart Studios Ltd.

**Library of Congress Cataloging-in-
Pubication Data:**
Herger, Bob.
    The coast of British Columbia.

    Includes bibliographical references.
    1. Pacific Coast (B.C.)—History.
2. Natural history—British
Columbia—Pacific Coast. I. Neering,
Rosemary. II. Title.
F1089.P2H47 1990   971.'1   89-17871
ISBN 0-88240-370-2

Printed and bound in Canada

Alaska Northwest Books™
22026 20th Avenue S.E.
Bothell, Washington 98021
A division of GTE Discovery Publica-
tions, Inc.

To my parents, Marj and Bill.
—B.H.

. . . .

To those who over the years have fought
and continue to fight to save the coastal
environment.
—R.N.

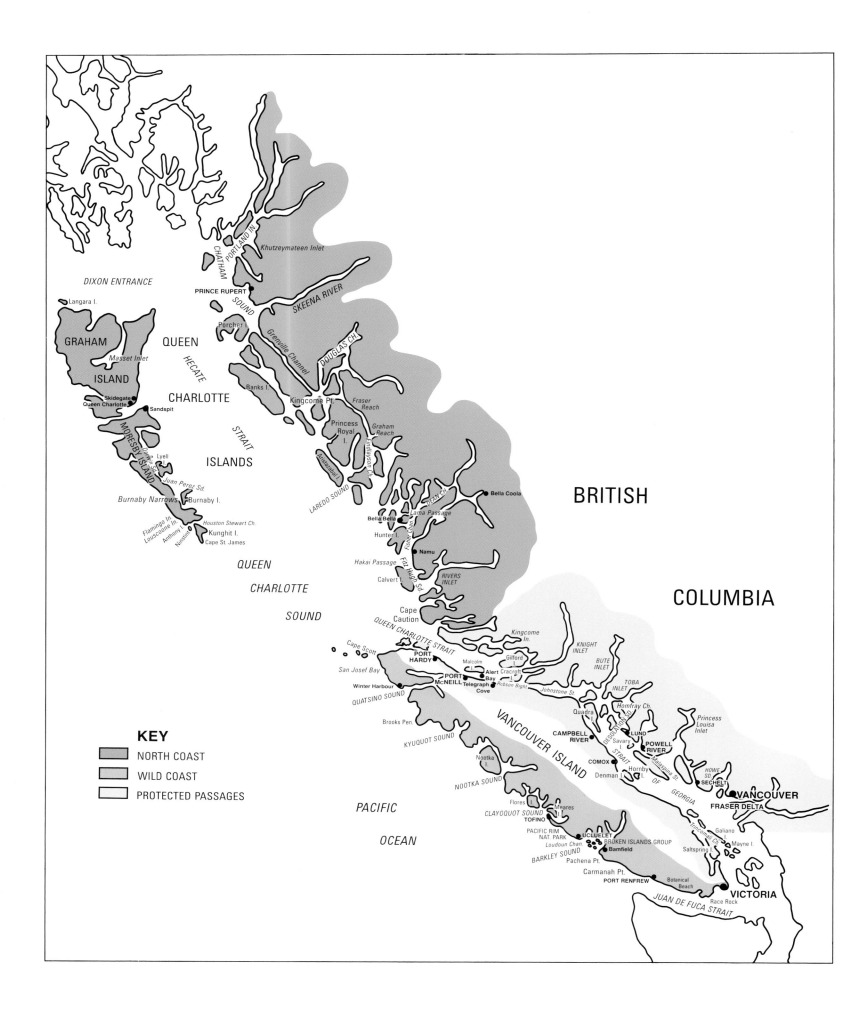

KEY

NORTH COAST

WILD COAST

PROTECTED PASSAGES

DIXON ENTRANCE

Langara I.

GRAHAM

QUEEN

ISLAND

Masset Inlet

HECATE

Skidegate
Queen Charlotte
Sandspit

CHARLOTTE

MORESBY ISLAND

Darwin Sd.
Lyell
Juan Perez Sd.

STRAIT

ISLANDS

Burnaby Narrows Burnaby I.

Flamingo In.
Louscoone In.
Anthony I.
Ninstint
Kunghit I.
Cape St. James

Houston Stewart Ch.

QUEEN

CHARLOTTE

SOUND

CHATHAM

SOUND

PORTLAND IN.

Khutzeymateen Inlet

PRINCE RUPERT

Porcher I.

SKEENA RIVER

Grenville Channel

DOUGLAS CH.

Banks I.

Kingcome Pt.

Fraser Reach

Princess Royal I.

Graham Reach

Findlayson Ch.

Abtsazabbal

LAREDO SOUND

DEAN CH.

Lama Passage

Bella Bella

Fisher Chan.

Hunter I.

Namu

Hakai Passage

Calvert I.

Fitz Hugh Sd.

RIVERS INLET

Bella Coola

BRITISH

COLUMBIA

Cape Caution

QUEEN CHARLOTTE STRAIT

Cape Scott

San Josef Bay

PORT HARDY

Winter Harbour

PORT McNEILL

QUATSINO SOUND

Malcolm

Alert Bay

Cracroft I.

Telegraph Cove

Robson Bight

Johnstone St.

Kingcome In.

Gilford

KNIGHT INLET

BUTE INLET

TOBA INLET

Homfray Ch.

Quadra I.

DESOLATION SD.

Savary I.

LUND

Princess Louisa Inlet

Brooks Pen.

KYUQUOT SOUND

VANCOUVER ISLAND

CAMPBELL RIVER

POWELL RIVER

COMOX

Hornby I.

Denman I.

Malaspina St.

STRAIT

OF

GEORGIA

HOWE SD.

SECHELT

Nootka I.

NOOTKA SOUND

Flores I.

Meares I.

CLAYOQUOT SOUND

TOFINO

PACIFIC

OCEAN

PACIFIC RIM NAT. PARK

Loudoun Chan.

BARKLEY SOUND

UCLUELET

BROKEN ISLANDS GROUP

Bamfield

Pachena Pt.

Carmanah Pt.

PORT RENFREW

Botanical Beach

VANCOUVER

FRASER DELTA

Galiano I.

Trincomali Ch.

Mayne I.

Saltspring I.

VICTORIA

Race Rock

JUAN DE FUCA STRAIT

C O N T E N T S

Bob Herger was seven years old when he discovered the coast. His family travelled from its Burnaby home in its new 1956 Dodge to the long sandy reaches of Boundary Bay. Not an epic adventure for anyone but a seven-year-old, but Herger can still remember the grittiness of the sand, the wash of the waves. Fixed in his mind is the moment when he turned back toward shore after walking out forever across the wave-ridged beach uncovered by the retreating tide, and saw far in the distance the black dots that were the rest of his family. He felt, not lost, not fearful, but happily secure in the broad expanse of coastal landscape.

The feeling never left. Instead, it grew to a love for the coast in all its aspects, from the peaceful sand to the crashing waves of a west coast winter storm. With his family, he has travelled the coast from the U.S. border in the south to the Alaska Panhandle in the north, by car, on foot, by kayak, by canoe, under sail, by air. For years, Bob has photographed the coast, knowing that one day the photographic images he was collecting would become the basis of a book.

Behind the images are the stories. A solitary orca cruises, black fin aloft, past rocks where stellar sea lions flipper themselves back from danger at the water's edge. A moment later, the orca closes in and grabs an unwary sea lion, tossing it almost playfully into the sea, where it is dragged beneath the water and drowned. The rest of the sea lions panic, and seek safety away from the rocks, in the water. Then the entire pod of orcas whistles in to prey on the sea lions.

If, as Bob insists, he has been lucky to be able to take these photographs, it has been a kind of "lucky in love." His own love of the coast has enabled him to portray its visual magnificence.

....

I first discovered this coast when I was nineteen and thought I would never stay anywhere for very long. Now I find to my amazement that I have been on the coast for almost twenty-five years.

The thought of living elsewhere moves me to dismay. The winds, sky changes and sea have entered my consciousness and will not be removed. As it has been for Bob, travelling the coast of British Columbia has been for me a never-ending process of discovery.

What stands out for me in the history of the coast is the ever-increasing pace of change. It took several million years to create the natural environment, several thousand years of native prehistory in which that natural environment was almost unchanged, and just 200 years for us, the immigrants, to make massive and irreversible changes.

And change goes on. Some is part of the natural ebb and flow of tides and seasons. Some is not. Some stares at me from photographs of oil-soaked and dying birds, televised arguments over river estuaries marked forever by logging debris and bays streaked with pulp mill effluent, images of stark hillsides and coastal valleys stripped of their age-old timber. Those changes make me fearful that the things I love about this coast will no longer exist a generation from now.

I have tried to write about the processes, natural and human, that created today's west coast, and the changes that threaten it. Bob's photographs are a celebration of the beauty of the coast. We both hope that future generations will have that beauty to celebrate.

A C K N O W L E D G E M E N T S

This book was many enjoyable years in the making and would not have been possible without the help and encouragement of many friends and acquaintances. I am pleased to have this opportunity to thank the following people: Dorothy Butler, Graeme Stuart, John Burridge for his great aerobatic flying, Kyle Balagno, Keith Lemc ke and Steve Good from Custom Colour, Koos Dykstra, Brian McLeod and Diana Hall, Jim Allen and Bob Sutherland from Eco Summer, Brian Kelsch for making kayaking so enjoyable, Joe Tathum, Vlado Matisic, Vinetta Peek, Gunter Marx, George Jean and Brian King, Bill Cozens for showing me right from the beginning what good photography was, Bretislav Truncik, Kathie and Laurie Navrot, Mike Meegan, Bruce Obee, Mike Taylor, Joanne Gould, Wayne McCory for excellent bear knowledge, The Pettingers at Pacific Sands, Chandler Keeler at Quad Colour, Tony Smith and Susan Nickason for being great kayaking companions, Ian McSorley, Kelly Brooks, Dean Morrisette, Kathy Dauncey, Elaine Jones for all the ideas for the foundation of this book, Brian Johnson for being such a loyal client, Tony Owens and Brian McGill, Bill Herger, Jr., Jim Haberl, Barb Souther for being a caring leader and for her wonderful information on the coast, Colleen MacMillan, the publisher of this book, lovingly seeing it through to completion, Brad Nickason, the designer, for all those times we walked the beaches thinking one day we would be able to do this book together, Dave Freeze from Adventure Canada for the Ocean Visions charters, and Tom Ellison who I met one rare sunny day standing on a wharf in the Queen Charlottes. With his boat the *Ocean Light* he took me places I would not have been able to discover. This book would not have been the same without his generosity, knowledge, and friendship. Thanks to our children Carolyn, Natalie, and Stephie for all the patience they've shown while I was taking one last shot. And to all who are fighting to save the environment, your hard work and dedication is appreciated. Lastly to Megan, the best of the best travelling companions, who over the years has kept me on course and showed great support and enthusiasm for this project. Thanks to all.

B.H.

Thanks for their assistance to Cliff Bancroft, Brenda Dixon, Vicky Husband, Peter McAllister, John Sansom, Bruce Whittington of *The Field-Naturalist*, and Cameron Young.

R.N.

THE
CHANGING
COAST

....

Carry yourself back in time 150 million years and watch the beginning of a time-lapse film, speeded up immensely from reality. The coast we know today is just beginning to evolve. Over a multi-million-year period of extremely violent volcanic activity, lava flows across ocean troughs and blisters out under smooth rock caps. The earth's crust ruptures and buckles to form mountain chains, and the

....

Left: *An aerial view of the Vancouver Island mountains, overlooking Toquart Bay and Barkley Sound, near Ucluelet.*
Above: *West coast surge channel.*

1

Reminders of the Ice Age

The mountain landscape overlooking the west coast gives ample evidence of ice ages tens of thousands of years ago. Steep-sided cirques exist where glaciers first formed; as the thickening ice moved down the mountain slope, it scoured out glacial headwalls to create these semi-circular indentations in the mountain peaks. Arêtes—narrow, knife-edged ridges—separate the cirques. Snow stays year-round on the north-facing slopes of the summits, which were sharpened by the erosion caused by alternating freezing and thawing.

great tectonic plates of earth and ocean slide and squeeze against each other. Action, volcanic and tectonic, combines to thrust the mountains of the coast and Vancouver Island upward, and to create the building blocks for the Pacific coast we see today.

Images on the film whirl past: change is now measured in thousands, not millions of years. Heavy snow falls for centuries. Snowpacks build in the Arctic, then further and further south. The snow is compressed by its own weight into mighty glaciers that spread across most of Canada. The ice melts; the glaciers retreat. Several times more, snow falls, glaciers form, ice advances, ice retreats. Each new ice age obliterates most of the evidence of the earlier one. Some 25,000 years ago, the growing glaciers begin to push their way for the last time across most of Canada. Along the coast, sheets of ice up to 2400 metres thick build up over everything but the tips of the highest mountains.

The present-day Strait of Georgia is completely ice-filled; an ice-shelf extends 40 kilometres beyond the west coast of today's Queen Charlotte Islands. The ice persists for thousands of years. Then, as the climate warms and grows drier, the ice retreats, sending its meltwaters coursing through valleys to the sea.

This last advance and retreat of a great ice sheet change the profile of the land. As they advance, the glaciers catch up rock and gravel; the sandpaper-rough undersurface bulldozes across the existing landscape, scraping smooth, rounded mountains into steep-sided peaks, and widening and deepening valleys. As the ice retreats, meltwaters flow down the newly widened valleys to feed a rising sea. Relieved of the great weight of ice, the land, too, begins to rise. Because the sea rises faster than the land, the line of the coast moves further inland than it is today; in some places it is as much as 300 metres higher than today's sea level.

By some 6000 to 5000 years ago, the ice has shrunk back to glaciers high on the mountainsides, and the coast at last looks familiar to a modern eye. Yet change, however gradual, is still going on. Today, most of the glaciers along the coast are slowly receding, and geologists think the coast is still rising, though at a pace infinitesimally slow.

. . . .

The coastal zone, thus formed, has three major elements: sea, land, and the area belonging to neither and to both—the intertidal. Though the boundaries of the sea have changed over time, the sea itself is the oldest element; its lifeforms have become infinitely complex over the millions of years they have taken to evolve. The great age of the Pacific Ocean, its water temperature and salt content, nutrients entering the sea from river estuaries, the ocean's currents and the profile of its floor allow the British Columbia coast to support a wealth of plant and animal life unequaled among the temperate coasts of the world.

As elsewhere in the ocean, the key links in the coastal undersea chain are the microscopic plankton that make up more than ninety-nine per cent of life below the waves. Billions of simple algae plants share space with a myriad of minute animals, most of them crustaceans similar in form to their much larger cousins, the shrimp. Larger plankton, barnacles, shrimp, clams and small fish feed on smaller plankton; larger fish eat smaller fish and shellfish; still larger fish and sea and land mammals feed on these.

Off the British Columbia coast, these chains, all beginning with the microscopic plants and animals of the ocean, link through the fish in the sea (herring, needlefish and oolichan to cod and shark and salmon) to seabirds and shorebirds, to sea mammals such as whales, seals and sea lions, and land mammals such as grizzly bears, and to man, the greatest predator.

The daily ebb and flow of the ocean tides define the intertidal zone. Once each lunar day, the tides repeat themselves; twice in each period, the waters flow high onto the beach and ebb back to their low. Between high and low water is the intertidal zone—in fact, a number of different zones, each defined by the length of time under or above water.

Just below the low tide line, where they can be underwater most of the time, are the carnivorous sea anemone, the spiny sea urchin, long ribbons of kelp and the native oyster, plus the larger oyster introduced from Japan in the 1930s.

Close to one hundred species of sea stars inhabit the coast between California and Alaska, almost five times as many as on the Atlantic coast. These sea stars, in brilliant purples and oranges, live at the low tide line. In ascending order towards the high-water mark live shellfish such as mussels and chitons, barnacles, limpets and species of seaweed. At the high tide line, underwater for only a few minutes each day, rock crabs scuttle along and spiral-shelled periwinkles inch at slothful speed. Beyond the reach of the tide is the splash zone, touched by salt spray and wave splash; here algae and lichens cling to rocks and driftwood. Throughout the intertidal zone, clams, marine worms, snails, sand hoppers and mud shrimps burrow below the surface, choosing hard-packed sand or softer mud, depending on their burrowing ability and speed.

Tied into the cycle of marine and intertidal life are the coastal birds. Ubiquitous, seagulls scavenge along the regions covered and uncovered by the tide. Freshwater nesters such as ducks, geese and swans visit the coast to feed on marine plants and fish. Bald eagles, nesting at the tops of spar trees overlooking the ocean, steal seabird eggs and scavenge from smaller birds.

Other birds belong truly to the sea, nesting on rocky crags and untenanted islands in giant colonies that echo with the cries of fledglings every year. Thousands of murres, guillemots, murrelets, auklets, cormorants, puffins and petrels wheel, dive and skim the ocean surface along the coast.

Beyond the reach of the tides, but within the compass of the salt ocean air, the coastal forests rise. The forest story begins with the end of the last ice age. As the ice retreated, seeds that had somehow survived the ice or that were borne by wind from unglaciated areas took root in the inhospitable sand, gravel and rock left behind as glacial debris. Probably the first to germinate were the seeds of the shore pine, a stunted tree that today still clings to land or rock where no other species can survive. The growing roots of the shore pine held in place glacial debris that might otherwise have been swept into the ocean by rain and glacial meltwaters. The pines grew, died and decayed; the humus they created combined with the glacial sediments to form fertile soil for other trees.

The shore pine could not compete with these newcomers that grew faster, taller and stronger than the first arrival. The Sitka spruce found its niche at the outer edge of the coast, where salt spray splashed the ground and provided the magnesium it needed for survival. In many places just further inland, the Douglas fir (a false fir that is actually related to the hemlock) took hold. In upwards to a thousand years, the Douglas firs—the largest trees in the coastal forest—grew to maturity, rising to 100 metres and growing to five metres in diameter. But Douglas fir seedlings could not tolerate the shade, and could not grow below the canopy of the nigh branches of the parent trees.

Now, protected by the shade and nurtured by the rotting logs of

Dowitchers on the Shore

Shore birds skitter back and forth across the sandy flats, working the tidal debris for food. Dowitchers, part of the same large family that includes sandpipers and sanderlings, work like little sewing machines, their beaks thrusting up and down and up and down like a needle punching through cloth. They have bills that are flexible at the tip; this allows them to probe deeper into the sand and to feel around for the small crustaceans and worms that make up their diet. Dowitchers breed in the Arctic, mostly in Alaska and Siberia, then fly south to Mexico where they winter. They stop en route on Canada's west coast during September and October.

Above: Dowitchers on the tidal flats.

Mussels and Middens

Shellfish such as mussels have long been a food source for the people of the coast. Left behind in ancient refuse heaps called middens, shells have provided one good way of measuring the length of time that a site has been occupied. They can also provide a record of the changing elevation of the sea; shells have been found embedded in rock far above the present-day sea level. Today, blue-shelled mussels are the most visible of the shellfish species, anchored by thin threads of protein to rocks and pilings revealed by falling tides. They live in the mid-tide zone, filtering tiny plankton from the water, each mussel filtering some fifty-five litres of water every day to build shell and the body inside the shell.

Above: Mussel shells, Lismer Beach, in Pacific Rim National Park.
Right: Children playing in the surf, Florencia Bay.

fallen trees, shade-loving conifers such as western red cedar, western hemlock and amabilis fir grew up. Because they could live in the shade of their own species, these trees reproduced themselves. The forest had now reached its climax stage, where trees of the same species would continue to grow generation after generation, until some natural or man-made change destroyed the forest.

By approximately 4000 years ago, the Douglas fir, the Sitka spruce, the hemlock, now so dominant in the west coast landscape, were all firmly established in a thousand-year cycle of change and growth. Perhaps every hundred years, fire would strike a portion of the forest, destroying the old trees and opening that part of the land to sunlight again. The cycle would repeat itself: Douglas fir yielding in time to cedar and hemlock. Lichens, ferns and mosses, among the oldest plants on earth, adorned the growing trees. Where sunlight broke through to the forest floor, a jungle of salal and young alder grew.

Though the tree species existed elsewhere in the world, nowhere did conditions favour them so greatly. Winds sweeping over the warm ocean currents picked up great quantities of water. The winds reached the island or coast mountains and were forced sharply upward; the cooling air dropped its moisture on the slopes of the mountains and the coast below. The rain fell mainly in the winter, timing ideal for conifers and inimical to deciduous hardwoods. Abundant rain and moderate climate combined with the trees own long-livedness to create a forest unmatched in grandeur.

Among these forest giants lived the land mammals. Bear, cougar, elk and deer; otter, raccoon and beaver; rabbit, mouse and vole: all lived between the ocean's edge and the mountain top, part of the natural cycle of the coast.

· ·

The end of the ice age brought radical change to the clothing of the coast. But the change was not just to the physical environment. For the first time, human eyes now viewed the landscape. As the ice retreated, human beings advanced.

Since the earliest inhabitants of the northwest coast left no written record of their arrival or their life, their history can be deduced only from the sparse physical clues that have survived the intervening years. Since the seas were still rising when they first made their appearance, much of what was left of their coastal villages has presumably been hidden by the ocean. Only now are archaeologists finding cryptic remains underwater, in regions then land and now sea bottom. Informed speculation suggests that the first humans arrived on the coast 10,000 to 12,000 years ago, part of the great movement of peoples across the Bering land bridge through unglaciated Alaska, then through the newly liberated Yukon and continental interior.

From these travellers are descended the native peoples of the Americas. Some reached the Pacific coast, probably moving along the river valleys of the Stikine, Nass, Bella Coola, Skeena and Fraser, possibly in rude seacraft south from the coast of Alaska. By 8000 years ago, colonies existed all along the coast.

The resources of the sea were much as they are now; the new natives probably fished for salmon and the oil-rich oolichan and gathered shellfish. They made tools by chipping sharp edges in rounded beach or river pebbles. They gathered roots and berries, and, as far as can be told from bone remnants, hunted elk, deer and seals.

Eight thousand years ago, however, the coastal climate was milder and drier than it is now; the pollen record from that era indicates

Above: Biologists have been trying to re-introduce sea otters such as this one to the coast of British Columbia.

that red cedar was not common along the coast. The natives had to use other woods, harder to shape, to build small shelters of bark and wooden slabs hewn from tree trunks.

By about 3500 years ago, the coastal landscape had assumed its now-familiar form. The shoreline between rapidly rising sea and slowly rising land had stabilized, and the climate had grown cooler and moister. Cedar seeds drifting with the wind found fertile ground beneath the firs and hemlocks, and the character of the rainforest changed. Colonies of shellfish increased along the now unchanging shoreline, and the number of salmon entering the rivers every year multiplied. The natives of the northwest coast entered a new stage of development leading to the great native cultures of the coast.

These native peoples lived in constant contact with their environment. Almost all of their food came from the sea. Salmon was their greatest resource, but shellfish, oolichans, seals, sea lions, sea otters and whales were also part of the diet.

The soft, workable wood of the red cedar stood at the centre of their physical existence. Cedar served every practical purpose: the huge houses of the winter villages were made from split cedar planks; canoes were hollowed from massive cedar logs; cedar wood was shaped into bowls, boxes, paddles and tools. Shredded cedar bark and roots could be woven into baskets, hats, skirts, coats and blankets.

The relationship of these growing civilizations to their environment was as much a spiritual as a practical one. Both religion and art were strongly linked to the beings with whom the native peoples shared the land and the sea. In spirit form, the woodpecker guided the hand of the canoe maker; the whale hunt was both a spiritual and a material quest. Clan crests showed clans guided by the raven, the eagle, the wolf or the orca. A slaughtered bear must be honoured before it was eaten—if in fact it was eaten at all. In many tribes, those who ate bear flesh could not eat salmon for two months, lest the salmon be offended.

The original peoples of the northwest coast celebrated these beings in their art. Carvers created both religious and secular art, most hewn from cedar logs and planks. Northwest coast totem poles, in all their carved cedar complexity, combined great artistic skill and guiding spiritual beliefs. Powerful masks with the visages of birds or bears permitted dancers to take on the personality of the creature represented.

By the late eighteenth century, the native peoples of the northwest coast had developed complex and rich societies. On the west coast of Vancouver Island, the Nuu-chah-nulth, at 10,000 strong probably the most numerous of the west coast peoples, lived in two dozen villages along 320 kilometres of coastline. Alone among the coastal peoples, they hunted whales from their seagoing canoes. Like the others, they depended on the annual salmon runs and the cedar forests for most of their necessities, and on trade with others along the coast for their luxuries.

On the southeast coast of the island and on the facing mainland lived the Coast Salish peoples, inheritors of the Marpole culture, one of the earliest to flourish on the coast. Further north, the Kwakiutl lived their winters in villages of 500 to 800 people, tucked along sheltered bays on the shoreline, and spent their summers at temporary sites where salmon were abundant. Along the fjord-bitten mainland coast lived the Heiltsuk, the Bella Coola and the Tsimpsean, all with strong spiritual traditions and artistic accomplishments that linked them with the world in which they lived. And across the rough sea channel, on the Queen Charlotte Islands, ruled the greatly talented warrior artists, the Haida. Master seamen in their 25-metre-long cedar canoes, they too fashioned totem poles, masks and everyday objects that bound their material to their spiritual world.

Such were the first civilizations of the northwest as they faced the agents who would bring radical change to their lives and to the coastal environment.

....

The world of the northwest coast peoples was no pristine, egalitarian, non-materialistic world. Wealth counted; so did status. But the acquisition of wealth and status co-existed with a respect for the land and ocean that fed, clothed and housed its people. Resources of the land and sea were for direct use, and only secondarily to be traded for goods with other native groups.

In eighteenth-century Europe and eastern America, Europeans had imposed their own order on the land, clearing forests so they could plant crops, mining metal to make weapons, tools and adornments, and using advancing technology to make themselves less immediately dependent on the environment. They sold resources for money that would buy them other goods or services. The first Europeans to reach the northwest coast came to conquer nature and to profit by it, not to coexist with it.

As ever in the story of the Americas, promises of wealth drew these new explorers to the northwest coast. Russians, Spaniards, Englishmen, Americans, competed for ownership of the land, and of the resources that went with it.

They quickly discovered that the coast was home to the silky sea otter, with its fabulously rich pelt which soon became the world's most sought-after fur. By the mid-1780s, a scant few years after English naval officer James Cook first set foot on the west coast of Vancouver Island, at the place he called Nootka, a sea otter pelt fetched many times a seaman's monthly wage, and the cargo of one ship loaded with furs could make a fortune for the ship's captain and his backers. Wrote Cook in his diary, "The fur of these animals . . . is certainly softer and finer than that of any others we know of; and therefore the discovery of this part of the continent of North America, where so valuable an article of commerce may be met with, cannot be a matter of indifference."

Indeed not. The promise of wealth from this new fur trade brought more than 300 ships to the North Pacific over the next four decades. Sailors reached down to club the otters as they swam, curious, beside the ship's boats. Native peoples eagerly offered the furs to the ship's crews, in return for knives, axes, chisels, blankets and alcohol. So popular were the pelts that, by 1820, the trade was over. The sea otters were all but extinct in the waters off British Columbia.

Through the 1780s, Britain and Spain argued over who owned the northwest coast, while Russia looked on with interest from its trading posts along the Alaska coast. Once the territorial contest was resolved in Britain's favour, Spanish ships retreated south. As the sea otter trade declined, the British grew content to ignore their new possession and left the coast to its original inhabitants.

The seclusion could not last. Explorers and traders for the Hudson's Bay Company ventured across the Rockies, seeking a route to the Pacific and new fur-rich territories to supplement the fading fur resources of the prairies and Arctic. The establishment of the fur trade in northern British Columbia and the founding of Fort Langley on the bank of the lower Fraser River in 1827 began a process that would be important to the coast: fur traders discovered the salmon runs on the rivers of the interior. Traders in the northern territory of New Caledonia traded with the interior natives for the 25,000 fish needed to sustain each trading post each year. At Fort Langley, chief trader Archibald McDonald realized soon after his arrival that Fraser River salmon, obtained for "Vermilion, Rings and other Trifles," could be salted, barrelled and shipped and sold overseas. By the 1830s, salted British Columbia salmon were selling in the Sandwich (Hawaiian) Islands, though shipments to Britain were less successful. Without the salmon trade, Fort Langley might well have been abandoned.

Early in the nineteenth century, the men of the fur trading companies followed the Columbia River, not the Fraser, to the sea, and established their posts on that river. By the 1830s, it was clear that the expansionist United States would soon gain possession of the lower Columbia. The Hudson's Bay Company cast about for a new location for its Pacific headquarters. James Douglas chose a site at the southern tip of Vancouver Island, "decidedly the most advantageous situation, for the purpose, within the Straits of De Fuca." He based his choice on the resources he saw before him: a safe and accessible harbour, goodly amounts of timber for home use and for export, tides powerful enough in the main waterway to drive machinery, and meadows that would serve for pasture and for growing crops.

Though the Hudson's Bay men cut down trees to build their fort and a small number of English settlers arrived to clear fields and start farms, they had little impact on the coastal landscape. Nor did the arrival of thousands of prospectors en route to the Cariboo goldfields between 1858 and 1864. Fort Victoria was transformed into a bustling supply town and a few settlers farmed and cut logs for sawmills, but the coast was of little interest to the frenzied goldseekers, and of even less to the businessmen and would-be ranchers who followed them. The discovery of coal at Nanaimo, and at Fort Rupert, on Vancouver Island, brought the development of small-scale coal mining, but there was little other activity along the coast during the nineteenth century.

The twentieth century brought major change. Early explorers had been impressed by the huge trees that thickly clothed the steep cliffs and mountains rising from the sea. John Meares, a British trader who spent several years trading out of Nootka in the late 1780s, wrote admiringly of the potential for timber cutting, and considered that, "The woods of this part of America are capable of supplying with these valuable materials [spars for ship masts] all the navies of Europe." Timbers from the coast went into the building of the Northwest America, the first ship ever launched on the northwest coast.

Over the following 120 years, the slowly expanding populations of Vancouver Island and the southern mainland made small inroads into the magnificent forests of the coast. The first sawmill opened near Fort Victoria in 1848; others soon followed on island and mainland. Loggers and mill operators cut the most accessible timber first, trees growing near rivers or close to the coast, that could be manhandled to the water and floated to mills. These early loggers did not have the means to make use of timber less readily accessible. Even with horses and oxen to drag the giant logs to the water's edge, the forests could not be exploited. In fact, a mill at Port Alberni, near the island's centre and surrounded by heavily forested mountains, was forced to close for lack of timber. The problem? "The broken character of the country and the Smallness and Shallowness of the Streams."

Then came the power of steam. By 1900, the first steam locomotive was chugging its way along a short Vancouver Island logging line. Steam was succeeded by the internal combustion engine. Logging companies had never lacked the will to log and ship out the giant logs from the coastal climax forest. Now they also had the means. Chainsaws, logging trucks, tugs to boom logs down the coast, mobile steel spars and log loaders, self-dumping log barges: innovation followed innovation as loggers learned the most efficient ways to harvest coastal timber.

By the late 1920s, thousands of board feet of lumber were being shipped from the coast to the United States and other markets, and plumes of steam and smoke showed where coastal mills churned out pulp and paper. Through the 1950s and 1960s, into the 1970s, the operative words were harvest, profit and man-years of employment.

The years of massive timber-cutting also brought a realization that the forest was not infinite. Government and logging companies began to replant sites that had been clear-cut, in the hopes of regenerating the forest, though many complained that far fewer trees were being planted than were being cut.

Replanting could not restore the original landscape of the coastal forest. The rainforest had taken up to a thousand years to reach its twentieth-century state. In a way not yet thoroughly understood by forest biologists, the ancient forest formed an independent ecosystem, where wildlife habitat, forest regeneration, soil quality and the very species of the land itself were interdependent. If you cut the trees, you destroyed the system.

As forest companies ventured into more remote areas of the coast seeking the giant old-growth trees, people began to question whether another decade or two of employment in the woods could be justified when placed against the value of preserving what was left of the ancient forest. Planting of young seedlings, destined to be cut within a century, would not produce replacements for some of the largest trees in the world. Nor would it restore the watersheds and streams to their original condition; salmon and shellfish were affected by changes in streambeds and pulp mill effluent. The animals and birds of the coast that fed on the creatures of the sea and shore would also be affected.

The battles began: man-years of employment versus years of enjoyment. Environmentalists and others pleaded with government and the forest industry to preserve some of the old-growth forest; forest companies replied that they could not afford to save more than a tiny percentage of the trees in their tree farm licence areas. By the late 1980s, someone flying over Vancouver Island could see that only a small rim of uncut trees remained. Estimates suggested that under ten per cent of the old-growth Douglas fir and less than two per cent of the old growth Sitka spruce of the coastal forest remained standing. British Columbia was in danger of losing forever the remnants of the most magnificent forest in the temperate world.

The forests of the coast were not the only battlefield. From the first European exploration and settlement, man had seen the coastal environment as something from which he could profit. Resources seemed infinite and renewable. With the invention of safe canning methods, fish canneries were built all along the coast, and hundreds of fishing boats brought their catches to the company wharves. Millions of cases of salmon and halibut were loaded aboard ships, destined for export markets around the world.

There had been warning signs that the resources of the coast would not last forever. For centuries before the arrival of the Europeans, Nootka hunters had engaged in battle against the mighty whales that frequented the west coast of Vancouver Island, and natives all along the coast had hunted seals for food. Then, between 1850 and 1900, hundreds of sealing schooners cruised the same waters, taking tens of thousands of seals every year. By 1902, the sealing industry was dead. The schooners

Lichens: a Unique Species

Lichens belong half to the sea, half to the land. Half algae, half fungi, two plants in one, they live symbiotically in icy Arctic wastes, in hot dry deserts—and above the high tide line on the coast. Grey, green, orange or black, they form a thin coating on rocks, which they gradually break down, creating soil.

Above: Gull feathers and lichen on the rocks.

had sought their prey as far west as the coasts of Japan and Russia, and now the seal herds were gone. In 1911, the United States and Canada banned commercial sealing in coastal waters.

By 1850, European and American whalers were hauling vast numbers of whales on board. By 1868, whalers were operating along the northwest coast. Four years later, the whales were so scarce that the coastal whaling stations were closed. Encouraged by the respite, whale numbers increased—and so did the number of whalers. By 1920, there were few whales left along the coast, and whaling ceased once more. When whaling resumed after World War II, such refinements as factory ships and helicopters and sonar to track whales increased the kill. Within a decade, several species were close to extinction and worldwide efforts to save the whales were underway.

Oil spills posed the next massive danger to the coast. Tankers leaked millions of litres of oil along the coasts of Washington and Alaska. Oil washed up along the west coast of Vancouver Island took its toll, in fouled beaches and dead seabirds. Increasingly, the events of the 1980s have brought home to many the fragility of the coastal landscape.

So much had changed in just two centuries. That imaginary time-lapse film depicting the evolution of the coast has begun to move almost more rapidly than we can comprehend or control. If the millions of years it took for the mountains, seafront and natural life of the coast to evolve represent an entire week of film, then the two hundred years of European settlement can be shown in less than a second. Yet the changes that era has brought are monumental and irreversible.

The changes have affected some parts of the coast more profoundly than others. Although the first Europeans, arriving by sea, made their landfalls along the storm-lashed west coast of Vancouver Island, later immigrants scorned this rugged coastline; no cities were built here and no rail lines pierced the mountains to the coast. Yet settlement and logging and mining have had their impact; people now fight to preserve what remains of the old-growth forest along this inlet-indented coast and battle to slow the pace of environmental change.

By the end of the nineteenth century, the coastline along the protected passages between Vancouver Island and the mainland had proven the most attractive for settlement and development. It is here that change has been most rapid and most extensive. Yet even here, the beauty of the coast has sometimes held its own against spreading cities and encroaching industry.

Further north, on the jagged-edged mainland and the Queen Charlottes, lies the last truly wild coast. Settlements have been planted in this wilderness, but have failed to thrive; loggers have built their roads and miners dug their pits, yet still this coast most closely resembles what must have met the eyes of those first arrivals 10,000 years ago in real time, a minute ago in that speeding time-lapse movie. Here, more than anywhere else, exists a real chance to slow the pace of change—or to find alternatives to change—on the coast of British Columbia.

....

Right: *A seaweed-fringed beach and coastal rocks.*

THE
WILD COAST

……   ……

"**T**his dangerous group is appropriately named, for the tide makes a perfect race around it," wrote Captain Kellett of the surveying ship HMS *Herald* in 1846. It was a most restrained comment upon the dangers of the tides and currents that surge past Race Rocks, the southernmost point in British Columbia and the beginning of Vancouver Island's west coast.

The strong currents, unpredictable heavy seas and fierce tidal rips around Race

....

Left: Ocean breakers at wind-lashed Cape Scott, northern tip of Vancouver Island.

Above: Keyhole limpet shell and yellow creeping silverweed, Brooks Peninsula.

Intertidal Life

The rising and falling tides cover and reveal the multitudinous life forms that live between high and low water mark. At the high tide line, limpets shave off the film of algae left behind by the falling tide. In the middle tide zone, barnacles fan the water with their twelve hairy legs, to feed on plankton, then click together tightly as the water level falls. In tidal pools trapped in rocky enclosures as the tide falls, sea stars, sea urchins and sea anemones cling fiercely. Sea stars extrude their stomachs to engulf their prey; urchins chew algae with a five-toothed jaw; anemones sting then close their tentacles on the paralyzed prey and pass it to a centrally located mouth. Sponges, crabs, mussels, clams and many other plants and animals also inhabit the intertidal zone.

Above: Purple sea urchin and coralline.

Rocks provide an appropriate introduction to this coast. Unprotected by any intervening land from the full force of the Pacific waves and winds that build across the 8000 kilometres between Asia and British Columbia, the west coast of Vancouver Island is pounded by storms and sluiced with heavy rain through much of the year.

The southern coastal strip, from Rocky Point opposite Race Rocks to the town of Port Renfrew on the bay known as Port San Juan, has long been settled. The first residents were the Coast Salish, some related to the Salish of the mainland coast, some to the Clallam tribes on the Olympic Peninsula to the south.

The earliest European explorers made their landfalls further north, but also explored this southern coast. Manuel Quimper of the Spanish navy, commanding the captured British sloop *Princess Royal*, explored and named the points along this coast in 1790; the names of Port San Juan, Bonilla Point, and Sombrio and Jordan rivers are evidence of his endeavours.

In 1787, Charles William Barkley, captain of the trading ship *Imperial Eagle*, sailed into this area, where "to the great astonishment of all on board a large opening with a clear easterly horizon presented itself. The entrance appeared to be about four leagues wide and remained that width as far as the eye could see." Barkley had found the long-lost strait discovered—though few believed him—by Greek seaman Apostolos Valerianos, otherwise known as Juan de Fuca, sailing for the Spanish crown in 1592.

The first recorded white settler west of Victoria was Walter Coloquhoun Grant, a British immigrant who edged his way out from Fort Victoria in 1850. Grant was one of those British adventurers whose stories enliven colonial history. Perhaps his fate was set soon after his arrival on the Island, when he heroically faced and shot down a marauding buffalo—actually a peaceable domestic cow. He ran up debts, tried and failed to work as a surveyor, got into quarrels with the natives and with the men he brought with him from England, and in general proved that he was not cut out to be a farmer, gentleman or otherwise. He did, however, clear 14 hectares at Sooke, west of Fort Victoria, and build a sawmill.

The next would-be settlers came overland, from the east coast of the Island via Cowichan Lake to Port San Juan and the mouth of the Sooke River. En route, they discovered gold on the Leech and Sooke rivers. Though the subsequent gold rush was short-lived, it led to the building of a passable coastal road and trails from Fort Victoria to the Sooke River and into the hills.

Today's road follows the coast west and northwest from Victoria, through the farm and commuter districts of Metchosin and Sooke, on to the smaller communities of Jordan River and Port Renfrew. Parks, regional and provincial, are spaced out along the shoreline, some microcosms of coastal life, others such as East Sooke Park larger and wilder, or providing sand and rock flats such as those at French and China beaches.

Earlier visitors were not blind to the beauty of this region; near the turn of the century, University of Minnesota marine biologist Josephine Tilden hired a native guide to show her the coast, and to help her find the ideal location for a seaside station where biologists from around the world could study intertidal life.

Just beyond Port Renfrew, they found Botanical Beach. Sandstone pockmarked with potholes ground out by ancient glacial action and deepened by the pounding of waves shelved down toward the Pacific, covered and uncovered by each successive tide. Each pothole differed from the next; in each, a separate marine environment existed. Tilden was enchanted. She persuaded the state botanist of Minnesota that her dreamed-of marine station must be built at Botanical Beach.

A lodge and several laboratory buildings went up near the beach, and scientists from the United States and Japan came to study the intertidal life. The station lasted just seven years; then Tilden left for the last time "the BEST place in the country for a scientific study of marine life, both seaweeds and animals." Botanical Beach itself is now a Class A provincial park, its seaside treasures protected.

The road ends at Port Renfrew. From Port Renfrew north to Pachena Point is an unforgiving shore of waves crashing against vertical rock, storm, fog, strong ocean currents and deceiving tides. This stretch of the coast has long been known as the Graveyard of the Pacific; uncounted ships have ended their days breaking up on the rocks north of Juan de Fuca Strait. So many lives were lost that, in 1889, the federal government built a telegraph trail to link the lighthouses at Carmanah Point and Cape Beale with Victoria, so shipwrecked seamen who managed to struggle ashore could let someone know of their plight, and so that the lighthouse keepers could send word when a ship piled up on the rocks. For years a telegraph, later, a telephone line was maintained by solitary linemen who hiked the rugged trail through rain and fog, from cabin to cabin, each nine kilometres apart.

The most famous west coast wreck was the *Valencia*, an American steamship bound for Victoria in the stormy January of 1906. Somehow, the ship's captain missed the strait entrance and piled up on the rocks near Pachena Point. The ship's 164 passengers and crew abandoned ship for the lifeboats, but the pounding surf capsized the boats. Although all aboard survived the shipwreck, 126 people died trying to reach shore, making this British Columbia's worst marine accident. Rescuers who arrived a day and a half after the disaster could only look on as the waves broke over the ship and turned her decks-down to the sea.

The wreck of the *Valencia* convinced the government that the telegraph trail must be turned into a lifesaving trail, so shipwrecked mariners could reach safety and rescue parties could move swiftly to help.

Over the years, new navigational aids meant fewer wrecks and the brush encroached again on the trail, now little-used. In the 1960s, hikers began to clear the trail once more; it soon became known the world around as the West Coast Trail, a six-day adventure along the coast and through the rainforest of the Island's coast.

As logging roads snaked west and north from logged areas into the Island wilderness, more and more old-growth timber fell to the chainsaw. By the early 1970s, logging trucks rumbled dangerously close to the magnificent forest that bounded the trail. Environmentalists and hikers who wanted to preserve the area around the trail battled to keep it unlogged. Eventually, the trail corridor and most of the Nitinat Triangle, a wedge-shaped series of lakes and rivers between the coast and Lake Cowichan much beloved by canoeists, were included within the boundaries of Pacific Rim National Park.

The largest known Sitka spruce still standing on the west coast grow just outside the park boundary, in the Carmanah Valley. Here, the quintessential coastal trees, three metres in diameter, soar more than 90 metres into the air. As logging companies pushed ever nearer to the valley, environmental groups banded together to publicize and try to save the entire valley from logging. The logging company and woodworkers' union replied that it would cost too much, in jobs and timber, to save all of the valley, and offered to preserve just the section where the largest trees grew. Not enough, cried their opponents; to cut the slopes above the prize trees would desecrate the watershed.

The Forest Clear-cut

No logging technique raises such high passions as does clear-cutting. In a clear-cut, every tree in a section of forest is felled by saw or dragline. Those that are valuable are sent to mills or market; the commercially valueless are pushed together and, usually, burned over in a slash burn. Then new seedlings are planted in the bared earth.

Forestry companies claim that clear-cutting is the only commercially viable technique in many areas, that it is the best way of preparing the area for a new crop of trees, and that it does little damage to the environment. Environmentalists view the naked slopes left by clear-cuts with absolute horror. Rain washing down the slopes carries away valuable nutrients. Clear-cutting destroys wildlife habitat, and carelessly dumped slash and debris caught up in water runoff choke streams and river estuaries. Trees that would one day grow to harvestable size are torn down and destroyed, and the steep and unforgiving slopes often defy man's best attempts at replanting.

Above: Clear-cut logging slopes.

Carmanah became one more tug-of-war between the opposing forces of immediate economic gain and long-term preservation of the wilderness.

At the northern end of the West Coast Trail is Bamfield, named (almost correctly) for W.E. Banfield, a trader and amateur ethnographer, the earliest white resident of the area. The first protected anchorage north of Port Renfrew, the town is reachable overland only by logging road. Bamfield is bisected by the inlet. No roads exist on the west side; all movement is on foot along the waterfront boardwalk, or by boat. The town is home to forestry camps, bases for the logging that takes place between the town and Port Alberni. Three or four times a week, depending on the time of year, the MV *Lady Rose*, a 31-metre passenger and cargo boat out of Port Alberni at the head of the Alberni Inlet, chugs up to the floats.

Often to be found scrounging along the shore or cruising the inlet are students and faculty from the four western Canadian universities that operate a marine biology station at Bamfield. The universities inherited a cable station built in 1902, at the western terminus of the trans-Pacific telegraph cable. From Bamfield, the cable reached 6500 kilometres to Fanning Island in the mid-Pacific, then on to Australia, the final link in a communication system that encircled the world. The cable station was closed in 1959, made redundant by more modern systems of communication.

Just north of Bamfield, Barkley Sound cuts a wide rectangular opening into the coast. Leading from the sound, arms of the sea chisel eastward through the mountains, two-thirds of the way across the Island. Port Alberni, 50 kilometres from the Island's east coast and twice that distance from the west, is actually on an arm of the open Pacific.

The southern channel leading from Barkley Sound is named for the ship *Imperial Eagle*, commanded by Captain Charles William Barkley; the northern channel, Loudoun, bears the previous name of the Eagle, when she served as an East Indiaman.

Frances Barkley, Barkley's seventeen-year-old wife and the first European woman known to have visited these precincts, was not impressed by what she saw, and was happy to leave the Island's west coast for their next destination, China. They took with them 800 sea otter pelts; they left behind their own, their relatives', their friends' and their shipmates' names on sundry geographic features. They also left the bodies of some of the seamen: purser John Beale, the second mate, and a boat's crew were killed in a battle with Indians near Cape Flattery on the Olympic Peninsula.

The same advancing ice that carved deep channels that became sea inlets spilled vast amounts of sediment as it retreated. Time and tides ground the glacial deposits finer and finer, ocean currents lapped the sediments along the ocean front and wind and wave smoothed it into long, flat stretches between the rocky headlands. The result is the west coast beaches that lie between Ucluelet, on the north shore of Barkley Sound, and Tofino, on the south shore of Clayoquot Sound.

These long, flat, sandy stretches where the waves roll in with numbing regularity are unique on the northwest coast. Elsewhere on the coast, currents, waves and erosion create pocket beaches sandwiched between irregular rocky headlands that have resisted erosion for thousands of years. Most of the other long, sandy beaches on Canada's

. . . .

Left: *The freighter Lady Rose unloads cargo at Gibraltar Island, at the head of Alberni Inlet, while kayakers stop by.*

Above: Crab traps at Tofino, with Meares Island in the background.

west coast are the result of river-borne sediment deposited at river mouth. Almost twenty years ago, the province and the federal government recognized the uniqueness of this area and agreed that a national park should be created to protect this special environment.

Environmentalists and others wanted to see more protected than just the beaches; they sought preservation of an ecological zone that included beach, dunes and old-growth forest and inclusion of the offshore Broken Islands within the park boundaries. Logging companies that owned tree farm licences in the area were not averse to the idea; in return, however, they wanted equivalent logging rights nearby. But equivalent accessible old-growth forest on the Island west coast was rapidly disappearing; there was little land left to bargain with. Finally, the beach area, the Broken Islands and an underwater reserve were made part of the park.

Long Beach faces the only stretch of open Pacific readily accessible to British Columbians and visitors to the province. A good, though winding, paved road has replaced the terrorizing switchbacks of the original goat trail from Port Alberni through the mountains west, and neat campsites are now laid out where driftwood shanties used to house peaceful hippies. Signs now planted along the beach to warn against rogue waves and tide changes might have helped visitors in previous years who drove their cars over the sand and sometimes lost them to the vagaries of shifting tides.

For many of the thousands of visitors who come here every year, Long Beach is their first close-up encounter with the real ocean. Endless waves roll onto the patterned sand, grey whales cruise offshore in February and March, sea lions sun themselves on wave-splashed rocks, bright purple and orange sea stars cling to rocks at the limits of the beaches, and geese and eagles wheel in the sky. Herons stalk the shallows and sandpipers skitter along the beach.

Just beyond the northern boundary of the park sits the fishing village of Tofino, at the south end of Clayoquot Sound. Offshore lies Meares Island. Home for 5000 years to natives, it was to them a special place for vision quests and ancestral burials. It was renamed in 1862 for John Meares, an eighteenth-century west-coast trader who could serve as a supreme example of the new capitalist. Shrewd, unscrupulous, energetic, prepared to lie convincingly for private profit or public glory, Meares managed to wangle a sizeable payment from the Spanish government for the seizure of his ships and the loss of trade he suffered at the hands of the Spanish at Nootka Sound.

In 1980, the forestry company that had logging rights to the island presented its logging plan as a matter of course to the provincial government. Public response was immediate and negative. The Clayoquot Indian Band filed a land claim with the Supreme Court of Canada, saying they had never given over title of the island; they declared it a tribal park, the first such in British Columbia, to be preserved for future generations. In 1984, as the logging company sent loggers by boat to the island, environmentalists threw themselves in front of the logging equipment, declaring they would stop at nothing to save the trees of Meares, among them some of the largest cedars in Canada. When the logging company announced it planned to cut 100 hectares a year for thirty-five years, and that it would leave a strip opposite Tofino unlogged, to preserve the view for tourists and residents, the opposing coalition was unmoved. On Meares, the conflict between immediate profit and employment and long-term preservation was clear.

Beyond Tofino, no roads exist along the now deeply incised coast; travel is by boat or float plane. Small boats rendezvous at Hot Springs

Cove, in Maquinna Park, named for the chief who led the Nuu-Chah-Nulth of this area in the late eighteenth century. This safe harbour with its stream of hot water tumbling down into rock pools and thence into the sea, is so popular that a regular float plane service now brings visitors from Tofino for an afternoon soak in hot pools and the occasional salutary splash from a chilly Pacific wave.

Isolated and little visited now, the coast north of Tofino has long been home to the Nuu-Chah-Nulth bands, known for many years to outsiders as the Nootka. The Nuu-Chah-Nulth were the most independent of the west coast peoples, isolated from contact with other native groups by the mountains that stood between them and the rest of the northwest world and by the fierce seascape to north and south. They needed little from the rest of the world. The land supplied deer, elk and other game, but the ocean was the basis of their existence. The Nuu-Chah-Nulth netted and caught in weirs the five species of salmon that spawned in the coastal rivers, and boiled or roasted them for immediate eating or air-dried them for winter supplies. Dogfish, halibut, sharks, herring, octopus and shellfish were also part of the ocean's bounty. Everywhere along this coast are huge shell middens, evidence of the immense number of shellfish harvested and eaten.

Alone among the coastal peoples, the Nuu-Chah-Nulth hunted whales. Each spring the hunters embarked in special whaling canoes, attended by rituals that ensured both luck in the hunt and respect for the hunted beast. Hunting whales larger than any Nuu-Chah-Nulth canoe demanded bravery; a man who was part of a whale hunt was greatly esteemed. The capture of a whale was cause for celebration and a feast where the whale blubber was shared among the people of the village and with honoured guests according to rank.

The Nuu-Chah-Nulth spent their summers close to the open coast or at temporary villages near salmon spawning grounds. In the winter, they moved back to their permanent villages in the sheltered bays and coves away from the winter storms. It was at Nootka, a permanent village on the north shore of Nootka Sound that they first encountered European explorers.

The arrival of Captain James Cook at Nootka in 1778 marked the beginnings of vast changes for the Island's west coast. Cook's ships left Nootka with sea otter pelts, beaver skins, and fox, raccoon, wolf, deer and bear skins. They left behind knives, chisels, iron, tin, nails, mirrors, buttons, other metal objects—and the knowledge of a different way of life where people looked at natural resources as a currency to be exchanged for other goods.

At the head of Nootka Sound, on Muchalat Inlet, is the pulp mill town of Gold River, linked to the east coast by one of the rare public roads that crosses the Island. For years, the *Uchuck*s I, II, and III have navigated the inlet and sound, carrying passengers, mail and freight to the outports and logging camps along its shores. One of the *Uchuck* III's stops is Tahsis, a logging and sawmilling town at the end of Tahsis Inlet, now faced with an industry inevitably declining with the ever-dwindling supply of timber.

North now again, no commercial boat or scheduled air service conveys people along the coast through Kyuquot to Quatsino Sound. Most who see these shores are sailors circumnavigating Vancouver Island or loggers en route to shoreline camps. If they are lucky, they may see creatures once extinct in these waters: biologists are trying to re-establish a sea otter population in Checleset Bay, at the north end of Kyuquot Sound.

Boaters heading north must make a jog here, around the strangely rectangular Brooks Peninsula. Brooks is an oddity on the coast, its

Right: Heavenly Grove, Carmanah Valley, home to the world's tallest Sitka spruce trees.

outlines out of place amid narrow fjords and jagged shoreline. Its geological history is the explanation: it is thought that Brooks was much less heavily glaciated than any other part of Vancouver Island, and that some parts of it may have escaped the ice altogether. Recent research has excited anthropologists and naturalists alike. The mountains of Brooks are relatively low and rounded and run east-west, not north-south like the other mountains on Vancouver Island. Many of the species of flora found here are unlike any others on the Island; many are endemic to the Queen Charlottes far to the north. Not far above sea level, Brooks is home to botanical species more common in the high alpine.

Anthropologists believe that a corridor along the coast of the peninsula was once above water, when the ocean level was lower than it is now. They have found ancient evidence underwater here, evidence that is valuable in reconstructing the story of the first residents of the coast. As often along the coast, environmentalists and others now confront forestry companies, as they try to preserve a unique area. Though Brooks has been declared a park recreation area, any mineral discovery on the peninsula in the next ten years could lead to mining—and the search for minerals could well result in roads being cut across the so-far untouched region.

North of Brooks, Quatsino Sound and its inlets slash across the Island to within 15 kilometres of the east coast. Roads reach out to the heads of most of these inlets, and evidence of industry is everywhere. An open pit copper mine operates at the head of Rupert Inlet, and tailings from the mine are gradually filling in the inlet and spreading out toward the inlet mouth.

Mineral resources at this northwest tip of the Island attracted attention almost a century ago, when Swedish settlers staked copper claims in the area. The area also has a romantic reputation, based on the foundered dreams of would-be settlers. Surprisingly, some such settlers chose the Cape Scott region, the most westerly point of the Island and one where weather can change in an instant, with wind rising from 5 to 45 knots in an hour. Danish fisherman Rasmus Hansen found a tidal meadow with salmon streams flowing through it not far from the infamous cape in 1894 and decided to found a Danish colony here. Promises and hopes ended in disappointment and failure; all that remains of the infant settlement are decaying cabins and meadows rapidly returning to the wild. Cape Scott and the land around it are now part of Cape Scott Provincial Park, with rough trails leading to wilderness campsites and beach walks along the rugged coastline.

Cape Scott marks the end of the west coast, that part of the Island slashed by glacier-scraped fjords and hammered by Pacific wind and wave. For thousands of years, its resources have supported the native people who make their homes along its sheltered bays and inlets. For two centuries, those same resources have been used in very different ways to support the new settlers of the coast. For decades, its forests, rocky coves and long sandy beaches have shown thousands of visitors the special wild beauty of a coast that faces the open ocean. What remains of that age-old wildness presents the greatest challenge to those who live on the British Columbia coast: preservation or irreversible change.

Dollars on the Sand

The bleached white or purple skeletons of sand dollars found on sandy beaches display little resemblance to other creatures of the intertidal zone—yet the sand dollar is a sea urchin. Instead of the eight-centimetre-long spines that protrude fiercely from sea urchins, sand dollars have spines only two millimetres long, crowded so closely together that the living creature seems covered in velvet. The five-petaled design on its back is another characteristic of the sea urchin family; you can see it through the spines in the living animal, but it shows up best on the dead creature found on the sand when the tide goes out. Sand dollars hate the turmoil of the surf; instead, they lie flat on the sandy sea bottom in tranquil shallow waters, or stand on end, a third below the sand, where a gentle current passes.

Above: Sand dollar skeleton, on a west coast beach.
Right: Bartlett Island, with Meares Island beyond, Russell Channel, north of Tofino.

The Why of Waves

The numbing regularity of waves rolling in from the open Pacific hides an important fact: no two waves are identical. The force of the wind, movements of the earth's crust, earthquakes, the movement of the sun and moon, the passage of ships, the depth of the water: all contribute to the size and type of waves.

Each wave begins as one of many forces breaks the undisturbed state of the water. Then gravity or surface tension pulls the water back down. The water rises and falls and rises and falls, until at last each individual wave crashes onto the shore. It is not the water that moves at the speed of each wave; a wave is a package of energy that moves through the water.

Two types of waves are most familiar to boaters. Chop waves, caused by local winds, are steep and irregular. Swells are long and regular, transmitting energy from storms that may be many kilometres away.

Left: *Waves break onto the shore, west coast Vancouver Island.*

Left: *Sitka spruce, fighting to survive, west coast Vancouver Island. When a tree decays and dies, the snag that results serves as a home for birds and insects.*

Above: *Children playing in the warm waters left by a retreating tide.*

The Cat-Foot Fog

Poet E.J. Pratt was speaking of a different coast when he described the fog approaching on little cat feet. But coastal fogs are the same west and east; they creep up on unsuspecting boaters or shore watchers, engulfing the sea and the land in silence and turning it blind. Dense summer fogs of the west coast, heralded by the hoarse voices of the fog horns, are created when cold waters swell up from the ocean depths to meet warm moist air. These fogs may last for days—or may be dissipated as the sun heats the surrounding land. August is sometimes known as Fogust, since the hottest month of the year may bring as many as fifteen days of fog. By November the foggy season is over, replaced by endless days of rain.

Left: Fog rolling over the Treble Islets in Peacock Channel, in the Broken Islands group.
Preceding: Evening light, coastal rocks and waves.

The Shore Pine Story

Few who see these twisted, stunted trees growing in the peat bogs of Pacific Rim National Park realize that the shore pine is the foundation of the magnificent coastal forest. In time primeval, it was the shore pine alone that could thrive on the thin soil and clean-scraped rock left behind by retreating glaciers, where its roots held in place debris that might otherwise have been swept into the sea. The shore pines grew, died, decayed; their detritus formed humus that covered the bare rocks and allowed a root hold for the Douglas firs that replaced them in the coastal landscape. The shore pine could not compete with the firs, cedars and hemlocks that grew faster, stronger and taller.

Today, the shore pine thrives only in the wet acidic bogs of peat and sphagnum moss where no other trees can grow, or in the poorest, most weather-beaten spots along the coast. Though a shortage of nutrients and minerals stunts and contorts its trunk and branches, the shore pine refuses to give up: some coastal specimens are more than three hundred years old.

Left: Pachena Point lighthouse, on the West Coast Trail south of Bamfield.

Above: Shore pine grows, stunted, in bogs and along the coastal fringe.

Patterns in the Sand

The sand beach stretches into the distance, ridged in irregular patterns that are a photographer's delight. They seem created haphazardly, yet their formation is strictly dictated by the tidal patterns and shifting winds of each beach. They are known as swash marks, rill marks or different kinds of ripples, depending on where they are on the beach and on whether water or wind shaped them.

Swash marks are built up in the swash zone, that region where waves alternately cover and reveal the sand. Each wave has an irregular swash, or pattern; each leaves behind a swash mark made up of sand, debris and foam. Each successive wave rolls over part of the swash mark built up by the previous wave. The waves build up a pattern of marks usually seen most clearly on the drier upper parts of the beach.

Sand ripples may alternate dark and lighter sand. The waves tumble sand and sort it according to the size of its grains; different-sized grains are often different colours. Above the high tide line, winds sculpt the sand into distinctive patterns, with gentle windward slopes and steep leeward slopes.

Right: Swash marks in the sand, Pacific Rim National Park.

The Fishing Fleet

When Pacific salmon return to the coast to spawn, the fishing fleet puts out to sea, following the regulated season openings up and down the coast, to catch the pinks, sockeye, chum, coho or springs.

Each fishing boat presents a distinctive silhouette. The gillnetter lets out its net from a small single drum near the stern of the boat. The net is set across the path of the salmon; the salmon can swim partway through the net, but then catch their gills on the net as they try to back out.

Like the gillnetter, the seiner lets out a net from drums near the stern. But the seiner has a triangular pole structure extending from the cabin, used to close or purse the seine net at the bottom once the salmon are in the net. The net is then drawn towards the boat and the salmon landed.

The troller carries the commercial equivalent of fishing rods, with two main poles about the length of the vessel amidships and usually two more in the bow. When the crew is not fishing, the rods are carried upright; when fishing begins, the rods are lowered to a 45° angle, and stainless steel lines with lures or baited hooks attached are dragged through the water.

Left: Fishing fleet, Tofino harbour, with Meares Island beyond.

Above: Western hemlock and Sitka spruce in the mist near Bamfield.

King of the Kelps

Though it is never noted in common usage, seaweeds are algae, those simple plants with only one or two different types of cells. Bull kelp is one of the largest west coast seaweeds, growing to twelve metres in length in a single season. The stalk, or stipe, ends in a holdfast that glues it to a rock or other solid anchor. At the end of the stipe is a float that permits the plant to wave near the surface of the water, so it can receive the light it needs for photosynthesis. Bull kelp has many uses: to clarify beer, to keep such mixtures as toothpaste smooth, and for sweet pickles. In general, however, west coasters scorn all seaweeds as food, leaving them to east coast Canadians and the Japanese.

Above: *Bull kelp floating in coastal waters.*

Right: *A commercial troller, poles at rest, enters Van Nevel Channel in front of Dead Man Islets.*

Above: Yellow loosestrife and horsetail fern.

Right: Tidal pools at Botanical Beach, near Port Renfrew.

The Simple Life

Among the inhabitants of the rainforests are some of the world's simplest plants. Mosses and liverworts are the most basic of plants, lacking roots and leaves. Next come the ferns, the oldest known vascular plants, with roots, stems and leaves but reproducing by spores and not by seeds. As attested to in the fossil record, ferns have existed for up to four hundred million years and grow in almost every part of the world. Horsetails, perennial herbs that have characteristic whorl patterns in their tiny leaves and branches, are very common and tolerant of poor soil conditions. Bracken prefers cool woods.

The Sitka Spruce

Alone among the rainforest trees, the Sitka spruce survives within the compass of the salt ocean spray. When it grows where the storm waves end, sea winds and spray mould it to a stunted windbreak known as krummholz. Behind these front line trees, the Sitka spruce grows straighter and taller, to an average of two metres in diameter and sixty metres in height. It is thought that these trees flourish where they do because the salt spray brings the extra amounts of magnesium the Sitka spruce requires. Where spray and wind do not reach, the spruce in general does not grow.

Left: *Sitka spruce in a January storm, near Winter Harbour, Quatsino Sound.*

Following: *Wind-carved sand ripples, Schooner Cove, near Long Beach.*

Barnacles

Barnacles are the most tenacious of the intertidal animals. They begin life as tiny swimming larvae. As adults, they cement themselves to rocks or other solid, underwater surfaces so firmly that they will never be able to leave—though the thatched acorn barnacle has a membrane at its base, and loses its grip more easily. Barnacles attach themselves so closely together that there can be up to 40,000 of them in a square metre. When they are covered with water, the shell top is open, and tiny legs sweep the water for plankton or tiny sea creatures. When the tide goes out, plates snap shut across the opening, trapping water within. The goose barnacle does resemble the neck of a goose but was named by sixteenth-century botanist and "amiable liar" John Gerard, who said that geese were born from barnacle trees, and provided chapter, verse and illustration on how and when the geese "spawne as it were."

Left: *Waves break over the rocks near Cape Scott.*

Above: *Thatched acorn barnacles cling to a rock revealed by outgoing tides.*

The Ubiquitous Gull

Their raucous cries are among the most familiar sounds of the coast. They follow the ferries, wheel above the beaches, sit in mysteriously arranged pecking order on pilings and driftwood.

It is almost impossible for the novice bird-watcher to tell one species of gull from another; in some cases, only the colour of the leg or the bill marks the difference between types.

The glaucous-winged gull is the only year-round resident of the coast, nesting here and wintering here. It lives happily beside man, scavenging in garbage dumps and following fishing boats to feed on debris dumped overboard. The other species nest inland, but, like many human residents of the interior, spend their winters on the coast.

. . . .

Right: *Migrating California gulls skim over west coast waves.*

Kayaking in the Broken Group

The Broken Group of islands, in Barkley Sound, has become an immensely popular destination for kayakers and canoeists, who prize the short island-to-island crossings, the ever-present beauty of the sea and mountain background and the relatively quiet ocean waters in the islands' lee. The group is part of Pacific Rim National Park and contains campgrounds designed for waterborne visitors. Some experienced canoeists paddle to the islands from the Vancouver Island shore. Others take the lazy way, loading their kayaks and canoes aboard the freighter *Lady Rose* for the trip from Port Alberni.

. . . .

Above: Skunk cabbage, bunchberries, deer fern and salal compete for space in a part of the rainforest floor where water collects.

***Right:** Sunset near Drum Rocks, Loudon Channel.*

. . . .

Above: Salal and salmonberry, west coast forest fringe.

Right: Purple and orange sea stars, green sea anemones, blue-black mussels and goose barnacles anchored to intertidal rock.

Salal, the Survivor

Anyone who has tried to make his way through the thicket of undergrowth that fringes the coastal rainforest can testify to the toughness of salal. This bush with the leathery, shiny leaves grows in jungly profusion, forming a thick, scratchy barrier wherever rain and sun encourage growth. Its white bell-shaped flowers appear in spring and are followed by black berries. Although the berries are not particularly tasty, they are abundant, and were made by coastal natives into syrup and into a dry cake that would last through the winter. Today, salal sprigs are frequently used in florists' bouquets, and a number of coastal residents claim the occupation of salal-picker.

Tides and Time

Medieval scholars suggested that tides were caused by an angel who dipped his finger in the sea, or by a whale that inhaled and exhaled the ocean. By the fourteenth century, scientists had measured and predicted tides with great accuracy, and in the late seventeenth century, Isaac Newton began the theorizing that led to our present explanations of the twice-daily ebb and flow of coastal waters. Since tides repeat themselves approximately every twenty-four hours and fifty minutes—the length of the lunar day—it is thought that tides are the result of a complicated relationship between the rotation of the earth and the gravitational pull of the moon. The greatest range between high and low tide on the west coast of Vancouver Island is just over four vertical metres, the usual range between two and three metres. Tides in the inside passages are more complex, since ebb and flood tides from several different directions overlap.

Left: Wave backwash, south beach, Pacific Rim National Park.

Above: Driftwood and Indian paintbrush, San Josef Bay, south of Cape Scott.

Above: Oil slick in a tidal pool.

Right: A worker assessing the effect of the oil spill examines oil-matted seaweed.

Oil Takes Its Toll

Three days before Christmas, 1988, a barge carrying heavy bunker oil overturned off the coast of Washington state. British Columbia coast residents trembled but were reassured that the oil would not drift north to the B.C. coasts. The reassurances were false. By mid-January, thick gobs of oil were coming ashore on west coast beaches, and by late in the month, it was clear that there was no adequate plan to deal with the effects of oil spills along the west coast. Hundreds of volunteers worked 16-hour days shoveling oil and oil-soaked debris into garbage bags; hundreds more tried, often in vain, to save oil-covered birds. Several thousand seabirds died as an immediate result of the oil spill. No one could predict how the oil would affect the food chain as eagles and raccoons ate the dead birds and as oil seeped into sand and rock. By summer, patches of oil were still appearing on beaches and residents asked how this spill or any other would affect the growing tourism industry on the coast.

Five months later, a major spill occurred in Alaska, and at last governments began to look seriously at ways of preventing oil spills and to realize that technology to deal with spills was seriously lacking.

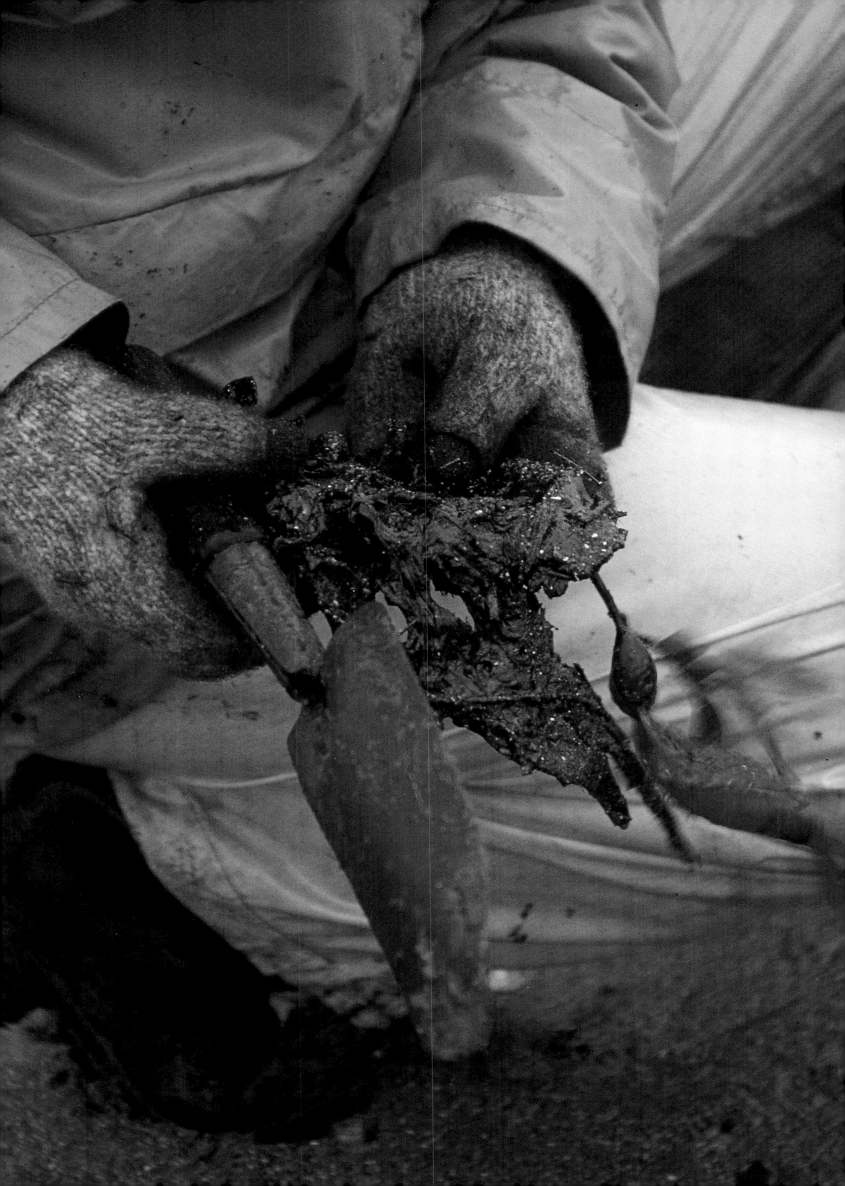

Weather Written in the Sky

In these temperate north latitudes, weather generally moves from west to east. If you want to know what tomorrow's weather will bring to the west coast, you can listen to weather forecasts compiled from reports transmitted from weather buoys at sea, ships and satellite photos to produce a prediction. Or you can look at the sky. Clouds appear in a rain-predicting progression: altocirrus gives a slight cloudy cast to the sky; horsetails of cirrus swish over; cirrostratus dim the sky; stratus, thick enough to hide the sun, cover the sky; then comes the rain. Then the sky breaks to cumulus or strato-cumulus, and fine weather returns.

. . . .

Above: *Clouds gather at the meeting point of sea and land.*

Right: *Kayaking at sunset, Willis Island, Barkley Sound.*

PROTECTED PASSAGES

The west coast of Vancouver Island shudders under the full thrust of the waves and winds of the open Pacific. In contrast, the east coast and the mainland facing it shelter behind the Island's bulk.

Winds deflected upwards by the Island mountains dump up to 4400 millimetres of rain on the west coast every year; by the time the winds funnel down toward the Strait of Georgia, they have shed most of their rainy burden. The east coast is much drier than the west, and some

....

Left: *Broom in bloom at Mace Point near Powell River, overlooking Malaspina Strait.*
Above: *Salmon fishing at Venture Point, Sonora Island, near Discovery Passage.*

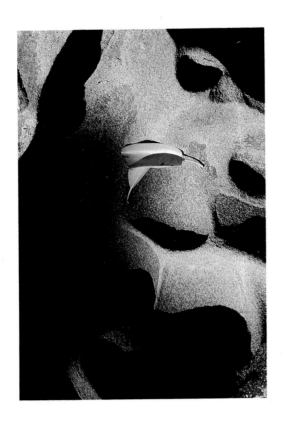

Above: Arbutus leaves and sandstone sculptures, Saltspring Island.

areas on the Gulf Islands are as close to desert as you will find along the coast, though the winds pick up more moisture as they cross the strait and drop it on the slopes of the Coast Mountains.

Gouging tongues of glacial ice fashioned a jagged coastline along the west of the Island, deeply indented by inlets. But the east coast of the island is relatively unbroken, and the southern section of the mainland coast is dominated by the wide, flat delta of the Fraser River.

In the earliest times of human habitation, the native peoples of both coasts used the resources of sea and land in similar ways. But with the arrival of European settlers in the nineteenth century, the destinies of the two coasts began to diverge. Protection from wind and rain, greater ease of travel, better land for a European type of settlement: all these factors made the inner coast more popular than the outer coast.

Each spring, two symbols of these changing destinies bloom at cliff-top above the sea on the south Island. Masses of deep blue spiky camass cover open grassy spaces; the flowers spring from tiny bulbs that grow wild along the southeast coast, and that were a favourite food for the Coast Salish. At the cliff's edge, in rocky crevices or sandy soil, deep gold clog-shaped blooms set alight the wiry broom bushes. Broom has grown here for little more than a century: the same Walter Grant who tried to pioneer at Sooke is said to have brought broom seeds back with him from the Hawaiian Islands. Like much else connected with Europeans, broom was soon acting as if it owned the place, colonizing wide stretches of the Island's south and east coast.

That we think this coast beautiful would probably have amazed the earliest settlers from Europe, more used to the wide fields of England, cleared for centuries. "The general aspect of the country," wrote Grant, "throughout the island from the seaward is particularly uninviting. Dark frowning cliffs sternly repel the frowning sea, as it rushes impetuously against them, and beyond these, with scarcely any interval of level land, rounded hills, densely covered with fir, rise high one above the other in dull uninteresting monotony."

Though not delighted, Grant was somewhat better pleased with the area around the Hudson's Bay Company post at Fort Victoria, built in 1843. "From these regions," he wrote, "which are wild without being romantic, and which, from the absence of any bold outline, never approach to the sublime or the beautiful, the traveler loves to descend to the smiling tracts which are occasionally to be met with on the seacoast."

Beauty aside, early visitors were not convinced of the utility of the region. "It is by no means inviting, in a utilitarian point of view," wrote naval surgeon Alexander Rattray in a book published in 1862. He suggested the soil on the hills was scanty and poor, and that little of the land was suitable for farming.

But Europeans had a long tradition of taming and using the land. At the southern tip of the Island, they set to work, cutting down the huge Douglas firs that dominated the mountainsides, using the resulting lumber to build houses and to ship home. Sections from a fir 92 metres tall were sent to England for the International Exhibition of 1862, and a 60-metre spar tree from the Island towered over Kew Gardens in London. It was the beginning of a logging industry that has dominated the Island economy almost to the present. Logging roads and railways pushed westward from the coast into the forests that clothed the mountain slopes. Pulp mills and sawmills were built, and freighters arrived to carry products to distant markets.

Yet a forest that once seemed inexhaustible was not. Loggers had to move further and further from the coast, into areas more and more difficult to log. Towns that once depended almost entirely on the forest industry heard with trepidation the news of mill closures and layoffs.

Coal was discovered near present-day Nanaimo and on the north end of the Island, and miners came from Britain to tunnel beneath the earth. Though towns such as Ladysmith, Nanaimo, Cassidy, Extension and Cumberland owe their birth to coal, the mineral had a short reign; by 1950, the mines were finished. Only crumbling mineshafts and pilings from deepsea docks where freighters once called for Cumberland's coal now testify to that earliest era of mining on the Island coast.

Settlers brought in cattle to graze the natural meadows and newly cleared fields. The fertile, rolling land of the Saanich peninsula proved the most attractive farmland; as that was taken up, would-be farmers moved north along the east coast, to plant the wide valleys at Cowichan and at Courtenay. But the farm fields that border the coast are now threatened by population growth that sees housing spreading year by year onto agricultural land.

The climate of Vancouver Island's east coast has encouraged more than trees. Refugees from sterner climes have discovered the coast, with its sunny days, warm ocean water and pleasant views of sea and mountains. Tourists have been equally drawn to sandy beaches and blue waters. Slowly, the east coast of the island is making a transition, from resource to service industries.

Offshore, in the straits between Vancouver Island and the mainland, lie the Gulf Islands, named in an earlier era when mapmakers referred to the Gulf, not the Strait, of Georgia. The more than two hundred islands are grouped in three clusters: the southern islands centred on Saltspring (the largest of the Gulf Islands), North and South Pender, Mayne, Galiano and Saturna; the central islands of Gabriola, Thetis, Kuper and Valdes; and the northern islands, among them Lasqueti, Denman and Hornby. The island names honour the English and Spanish explorers who were the first to map them. Saltspring, named for the salt springs on the island, is an exception. It started out as Chuan Island, derivation unknown, then became Admiral Island, named, John Walbran tells us, through the evident wish of their English surveyor, Captain Richards, to "associate the island with Rear Admiral Baynes, commanding at the time, 1857-60, the Pacific station, his flagship, staff and officers &c. He therefore named the highest mountain, Baynes, and the island, Admiral; Ganges harbour after the flagship; Fulford harbour after the captain; Burgoyne bay after the commander; Southey point after the admiral's secretary; Mount Bruce after the previous commander in chief; and Cape Keppel after a friend of Admiral Baynes." Walbran does not say whether Richards ran out of names, geographic features or desire.

The Gulf Islands were once part of Vancouver Island; thousands of years of wind, wave and rain eroded the connecting rock and dug the channels that set the islands apart from each other. In the rainshadow of Vancouver Island, the Gulf Islands are the driest part of the coast; on many, the availability of fresh water is the main factor limiting population. Vegetation is sparser and trees smaller here. Some plants that grow on the islands are found in few other locations on the coast. Most distinctive is the smooth-trunked, bark-shedding evergreen arbutus tree, known in the United States as the madrona. Its kinked limbs and reddish, peeling bark are familiar sights along the cliffs and sandstone formations of the Gulf Islands; Canada's only broad-leafed evergreen, the arbutus is native to the islands and to adjoining parts of the east coast of the Island. Similarly, the twisted, craggy Garry oak, the only oak native to British Columbia, finds hospitable terrain only on the Gulf Islands and the facing coast.

Humans are not the only creatures to find attractive the warm sunshine of the islands. Seals and sea lions bask on rocks at low tide, and

Above: Cockle shell at Boundary Bay.

the occasional pod or pair of orcas or dolphins breaks the surface of the water in Active Pass or the other waterways that weave between the islands. Seabirds such as cormorants, gulls, guillemots and puffins nest on the cliffs of the less-inhabited islands, as do the majestic bald eagles and great blue herons.

The islands are retreats where eroded sandstone forms fantastic caves and potholes, where rocky coves still provide room for solitary pondering, where nature, if not untouched, is at least unspoiled. The relative isolation, the climate and the beauty of the Gulf Islands each year attract more residents and visitors who come by ferry, private boat and float plane to escape the crowded city. For all these islands, the central question is, "How many people can live in a beautiful place without destroying that beauty?" How far development can continue is an open, sometimes acrimonious, subject of debate.

If you look at a map of the coast, you will see mostly white, blue and green. Only along the protected passages do red lines form a labyrinth of transportation routes and urban areas. The densest concentration of these lines lies at the mouth of the Fraser River.

The Fraser is the longest river solely within British Columbia, almost 1400 kilometres from its source in the Rocky Mountains to its mouth just north of Canada's border with the United States. Ice age glaciers widened the valley and left behind sediment that began to build the delta out into the ocean. For the past 10,000 years, sediment gathered by the river along its course has been deposited at the river mouth, building a widening delta and cutting new channels to the sea. The Fraser delta is the largest on Canada's Pacific coast, its valley the largest level, fertile lowland west of the Rockies.

We can guess that early man followed the valley to the sea; evidence that humans have lived here for thousands of years has been found near the Fraser mouth. Archaeologists have dubbed this the Marpole culture; their finds show that Marpole native peoples were probably the first representatives of the advanced culture created on the Pacific coast of Canada. They used wedges of antler and wood to split giant cedar trunks into planks, and basalt hammers and jade-edged adzes to build their huge plank houses. They wove mountain goat wool and the curly hair of domestic dogs into fine blankets, and cedar fibre into coarser cloth. From antler and soft stone, they carved images and figures that were probably used in religious ceremonies.

The first European approaches to the northwest coast were by sea; few travelled overland before the 1880s. These early travelers saw no advantage in clearing or settling on the thickly forested delta lands. Though the gold rush of mid-century saw the founding of towns such as New Westminster, for forty years, Victoria was in the ascendant over any mainland rival. When the transcontinental railway was pushed through to the coast in 1885, that ascendancy was over. From that date on, the human history of the coast centres on the steadily growing power and population of the Fraser delta and valley.

Thus, the delta lands, of all the coast, have been most changed by man. The delta provided an ideal site, first for agriculture, then for housing. Though land was set aside for bird sanctuaries and nature parks, it seemed unreasonable to expect any part of wild nature to continue to exist on this part of the coast. Yet the snow geese still return to Boundary Bay despite the nearby ferry terminal and coal port, salmon still come back to the river each year to spawn, and isolated pockets of coastal rainforest still stand within the urban boundaries.

The Fraser delta ends abruptly at Burrard Inlet; to the north, the coast resumes its more familiar form: a narrow strip of lowland backed by mountains that rise sharply from the sea. Explorers who found nothing to celebrate in these tree-clad mountains could not have predicted that one day, some of the priciest real estate in Canada would have been carved out of the steep and rainy north shore mountains that overlook Burrard Inlet and downtown Vancouver. For some, the phrase "west coast living" has come to be most closely associated with the high-style cedar houses of West Vancouver.

Burrard Inlet narrows twice; at each narrows, a bridge connects downtown Vancouver with the north shore. But the inlets that cut sharply into the coast north from here are wide and deep and difficult to bridge. No road crosses Howe Sound; now seaplanes, ferries and private boats must make the connections.

North from Howe Sound to Jervis Inlet lies a region dubbed the Sunshine Coast. Distant enough from the mountains to escape most of the rainfall that floods the slopes, the Sunshine Coast basks under some 2400 hours of sun each year, making it one of the sunniest places in Canada. This part of the coast, close to Vancouver, yet distanced by the intervening inlets, has attracted many who want both wilderness and civilization. Close to a hundred years ago, the Vancouver *News Advertiser* predicted this future, in an article about the first recorded visit of a Union steamship to Pender Harbour, on the Sechelt Peninsula: "Scarcely any place could be more naturally adapted for holidaying than this beautiful water which has the distinction of being the first land-locked harbour on the mainland north of Vancouver deep enough for ocean vessels." Known early in its history when all travel was by water as West Coast Venice, Pender Harbour is now built about with roads, but the feeling of a water-defined community remains. Around the harbour are some twenty marinas, marine stores and other businesses catering to boaters. The area has become a major attraction for divers, who explore shipwrecks and photograph the varied undersea life, especially during the winter when the water is least turbid.

The Sunshine Coast and the stretch of coast north to Powell River and the Malaspina Peninsula are half-and-half—half developed, half wild. Settlements, clear-cuts, logging dumps and booms, a pulp mill and other signs of development are visible along the road. Where the roads do not go, wilderness remains.

Though logging has denuded some of the slopes nearby, nowhere is the wilderness more magnificent than on the regal reaches of Jervis Inlet. Prince of Wales, Princess Royal and Queens reaches were all named in 1859 by the royalist-minded captain of the survey ship HMS *Plumper*; they commemorate King Edward VII, then Prince of Wales; Empress Frederick of Germany, the Princess Royal of England; and, presumably, Queen Victoria.

Mountains rise sheer from the water to heights of 2500 metres; the inlet floor drops just as sharply to depths of more than 200 metres. Though the immense scale of what they saw brought depression to early explorers, twentieth-century boaters have found no more beautiful cruising grounds than Jervis Inlet. Suggests mystery novelist Erle Stanley Gardner about Princess Louisa Reach, "Perhaps an atheist could view it and remain an atheist, but I doubt it." The Princess Louisa International Society, a group of yachters from Canada and the United States, owns part of the northern shoreline of the inlet, and vows that shoreline will never house any commercial operation.

When the early explorers spoke of the silence and stillness of these regions, they sensed but did not understand a fundamental characteristic of the fjords that break the coast. The wealth of marine creatures that make the west coast special is nourished partly by the nutrients that flow from river estuaries into the sea. Few significant rivers flow into the coastal fjords; the fjords are so deep that river water

Coastal Freighters

Vancouver's favoured location, at the mouth of the Fraser Valley corridor and just north of an international border, makes the city a major transportation centre. A wide, protected inlet provides a sheltered harbour where freighters from around the world berth, frequently anchoring offshore to wait their turn at the crowded docks. Products from the Far East—Japanese cars, Chinese silk—are offloaded and loaded aboard trucks and train cars; wheat, lumber and manufactured products go aboard for shipment to other ports. The walkway around Stanley Park, one of the world's largest urban parks, provides a convenient vantage point to watch the coming and going of commercial sea traffic.

....

Above: A freighter en route to Vancouver harbour looms up behind a lone seawall-walker in Vancouver's Stanley Park.

A People's Quandary

For many years, the Mamalilaculla band of the Kwakiutl nation lived at their village on an island near the mouth of Knight Inlet. Then, in the 1960s, the federal Department of Indian Affairs encouraged native peoples living in remote villages to move to larger centres, where it would be easier to provide services such as schools and hospitals. The people of Mamalilaculla responded; some moved to Port McNeill, some to Alert Bay or other points on the north Island, some to Vancouver and eastern Canada. But in so doing, they became off-reserve Indians and lost the benefits to which natives living on reserves are entitled. Some did well in their new homes; others were less successful. Now many band members, numbering about two hundred by federal government reckoning, or many more if you follow the native ways of tracing blood descent, want to return to their traditional isolated village.

Right: A weathered cedar pole at the abandoned Kwakiutl village of Mamalilaculla, near Knight Inlet.

that does enter the inlets stays as an upper layer of fresh water above the deep cold salt water. The inlet floor plunges sharply from the shore; only the narrowest of intertidal zones exists. The result: little microscopic plankton that is the basis of the marine food chain, few intertidal plants and animals, few fish—and thus, few seabirds and few land animals. The magnificent mountainsides that rise sheer and misty above the water and the deep green waters are all but devoid of life.

No wonder then, that Captain George Vancouver named the next inlet Desolation Sound, in despair at the "awful silence [that] pervaded the gloomy forests, whilst animated nature seemed to have deserted the surrounding country." Once more, what an earlier century scorned the twentieth century is learning to value. The sound and its islands and bays are favoured places for modern-day explorers who arrive in sailboats and motor cruisers, canoes and kayaks. The land around Desolation Sound tells its own stories of changing attitudes: abandoned logging camps and roads, apple trees gone wild and homesteads left to the forest, farm fields gone back to alder and salal. Man has tried and failed to tame this land.

Mainland coast, offshore islands and Vancouver Island wedge together now, divided only by narrow, twisting channels. From Desolation Sound north, the mainland coast is a maze of oddly shaped peninsulas, long deep inlets and islands fitted tight into the mainland. Once, promoters dreamed of a railway that would come to tidewater at the head of one of these inlets; one look at the map and no one could wonder that the scheme was never tested. Barriers of mountain and sea forbid the building of any system of land transportation.

The northeast coast of Vancouver Island is more forgiving, less forbidding. North to Campbell River, a highway follows the coast; then it curves inward along an easier route, to reach the northern coastal communities of Port McNeill, Alert Bay, Sointula and Port Hardy. For 8000 years, this has been the home of the Kwakiutl people; native culture thrives now again on the north island, where totems rise above traditional burial grounds and living museums at Cape Mudge and Alert Bay show the arts and traditions of the Kwakiutl.

Among the symbols of Kwakiutl art are those that represent the orca. A member of the dolphin family, the orca was unfairly known for many years as the "killer whale"—and is still defined in dictionaries as "ferocious." But increasing study of the orca shows otherwise: now hundreds of visitors come to the north Island for the chance to see the orca extended families, known as pods, playing, splashing and sounding in curves of black and white through the water. Robson Bight, at the north end of Johnstone Strait, has been defined as an orca sanctuary.

Queen Charlotte Sound widens toward the ocean and an end to the protected passages between Island and mainland. Man has found the most fertile land of the coast here, on river delta and valleys and on the rolling lowlands. Road and rail trace their way across this coastal landscape, and houses and industry sprawl from water's edge up the mountain slopes. Though the ancient trees are long gone and the secret coves and beaches all discovered, herons still wade the tidal mudflats and the whales still cruise the straits. Despite the massive changes, the beauty of the coast still pervades the protected passages.

The Peeling Arbutus

    The only broad-leafed evergreen in Canada, the arbutus, or madrona, is perhaps the most out-of-place tree on the coast. At the northernmost point of its range on the southern tip of Vancouver Island and the Gulf Islands, the arbutus is far more common in Oregon and California. It sheds its bark, but keeps its leaves through the winter; the long strings of peeling red bark reveal smooth new orange bark below. In May, it produces creamy white flowers in clusters, followed by reddish-orange berries.

. . . .

Above: An arbutus tree on the south coast.
Right: *Summer cabin facing Active Pass, on Galiano Island.*

Putting to Sea

Kayak, canoe, rowboat, sabot, catamaran, daysailer, yacht, runabout, motor cruiser: British Columbians own more than a quarter of a million boats, and 25,000 American boats cross the border headed north every year. Some days, it seems as if every one of those boats is at sea, its owners fishing, sailing, lazing, exploring the coves and inlets of the coast. With the growth in boating has come a growth in the industries and facilities that support boating. Marinas dot the coast from the border to the north end of Vancouver Island. The coast also supports a unique system of marine parks, thirty-one provincial parks intended mainly for those who arrive by sea. The first marine park was established on Galiano Island in 1959; since then, parks have been added to the system from Sidney Spit, near Victoria, to Desolation Sound.

Left: *A canoeist passes Paige Islets, Homfray Channel, beyond Desolation Sound, in the early morning.*

Above: *Government wharf, Savary Island.*

Below the Waves

For years it was a well-kept secret, known only to divers who lived near B.C. coastal waters. But the secret is out, and underwater diving has become British Columbia's fastest growing sport, now outstripping skiing in the amount of equipment bought each year and in the rate of growth. *National Geographic* magazine has said these coastal waters provide diving second only to those of the Red Sea. The major attractions are the startlingly brilliant reds and oranges of the underwater walls of coral, with mosses, fans, sea stars and other sea creatures clinging to them, and the variety of sea life that occurs in B.C. waters. It's rare in other waters, for example, to see octopus the size they grow to here. Hot spots for divers range from Sidney, on south Vancouver Island, to the waters off Powell River.

Left: A diver explores the underwater world near Telegraph Cove.

Above: A red sea urchin and sea star are attractions for divers on the coast.

Following: Sun-up, Lucy Point, Prideaux Haven, Desolation Sound.

Above: A British Columbia ferry entering Horseshoe Bay in Howe Sound.

Right: Eroded sandstone, at Dionisio Point, Galiano Island.

Story in Stone

The Gulf Islands are made up of sedimentary rock: sandstone, conglomerate and shale. Water and wind erode the rocks at different rates. Sandstone, the softest, erodes most quickly. Conglomerates are harder and less easily eroded. Erosion produces the fantastical galleries and honeycombs along some Gulf Island shores. Spanish explorers were the first to note these features; the Malaspina Galleries on Galiano Island are named for one such explorer. The cave-like creations scoured in sandstone here and on Gabriola Island are overhung with a roof of erosion-resistant conglomerate. They are the largest examples of the differing rates of erosion; in other places, the pockmarks are large enough only to house a cormorant's nest or to create a tidal pool.

The Forest Succession

As a tree ages, bacteria and fungi set to work, and the tree slowly decays. Eventually it dies and crashes to the forest floor. The fungi and bacteria secrete chemicals that digest the wood; millipedes come to dine and salamanders and toads make a meal of the millipedes. Mosses and lichens grow on the decaying bark; as the bark disintegrates, new trees take root on what has become a nurse log, where there is more sunlight than on the forest floor and a good supply of water and nutrients. Eventually, the roots of the new and growing trees will reach down to the forest floor; when the nurse log eventually disintegrates completely, the arching roots of the trees that grew on and over it will testify to its former existence.

One fallen cedar may provide a germination bed for thousands of hemlock seedlings in the hundred or more years before it merges with the forest floor.

. . . .

Above: Western hemlock seedling and Douglas fir.
Right: A beached and abandoned boom boat, Eliot Passage, at the entrance to Knight Inlet.

Left: Kayaking in George Passage, looking towards Malcolm Island, Queen Charlotte Sound.

Above: Burial ground, Alert Bay, Cormorant Island.

Harbour Seals

The quizzical, whiskered snout of a Pacific harbour seal poking out from shallow waters near shore is a familiar sight even in west coast waters close to cities. The harbour seal, a friendly and curious marine mammal, is an earless or true seal that feeds on fish. It's not much of a mover on land, because its hindflippers won't turn very far forward, but underwater, it's a marvel. It has been known to dive to depths of up to two hundred metres, and stay underwater for up to half an hour. Like others of the pinniped family, it exhales before it dives, then stops breathing underwater, where its heart rate slows and its oxygen consumption becomes extremely efficient.

Left: Harbour seal, Pender Harbour.

Above: Whale watchers photograph a passing orca from their tour boat at Robson Bight, near Telegraph Cove on the Island's east coast.

Communities that Look to the Sea

Where the road ends, the sea passage begins. Communities such as Lund, at the north end of the asphalt, look as much to the sea as the land. Even domestic geese forsake the farmyard for the water. Marinas and government wharves become the centre of activity, social and commercial, and craft ranging from commercial fish boats to houseboats to touring yachts and motor cruisers tie up so their occupants can acquire supplies and learn about weather or tides.

Above: *Sailors and domestic geese at dockside, Lund.*

Right: *Salal and memorial pole, old Kwakiutl village.*

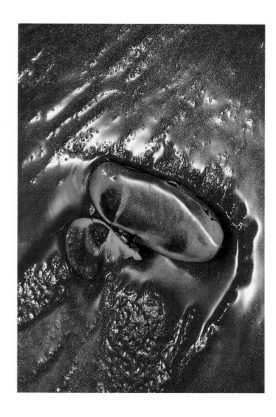

Left: *Manson Passage, between Hernando and Cortes islands.*

Above: *Razor clam shell in the intertidal zone.*

Above: *Two British Columbia ferries entering Active Pass between Mayne and Galiano Islands.*

Right: *Sandstone at sun-up, Tribune Bay, Hornby Island.*

The Orca

Some three hundred orcas, the largest members of the dolphin family, call the British Columbia west coast home. They live together in extended families called pods, with up to fifty but more commonly five to twenty members; pods group together in communities, each of which claims a separate coastal territory. Scientists who study orcas identify each one individually by the white patterns on their bodies and try to interpret the whistles, pulses and clicks they emit to communicate or to locate objects underwater. Orcas, which grow to some ten metres in length and nine tonnes in weight, were dubbed killer whales because they feed on both warm and cold-blooded animals. They will even attack Stellar sea lions, charging the sea lions and hitting them with their tails from below or above water for as long as an hour. There are no recorded incidents, however, of an orca attacking a human being.

Left: *View from White Cliff Islets, at the entrance to Knight Inlet, with Swanson Island beyond.*
Above: *Orca pods and seiner fishboat.*

Above: Sailing Trincomali Channel, in front of Wise Island and Saltspring Island.

Right: Dragonfly, Steveston, on the Fraser delta.

Dragonfly

A flicker of gold or green, a flash of wings silvery in the sunlight. The dragonfly hatches as a nymph in freshwater, then climbs onto a rock or plant and emerges from its nymph stage twenty minutes later as an adult. The green darner and the ten-spot libellula are common along the southern protected passages, where they feed aggressively on other insects, darting and somersaulting through the air in impressive aeronautic displays.

Cruising the Inside Passage

The twentieth-century city dweller values the beauty, serenity and majesty of the coast, and seeks its silence and the sense that here lies a country almost untouched by the furious pace of today's world. Each year, large cruise boats sail the Inside Passage bound for Alaska, on more than 125 return voyages between May and September. Luxury cruise liners with on-board spas, theatres and casinos offer top-of-the-pocket-book service, but there are also sailing charter trips for those who want to get a little closer to the coast's beauty, and frequent ferry trips between Port Hardy on Vancouver Island and Prince Rupert.

Above: *Fishboats head for season opening in Johnstone Strait, between Boat Bay and West Cracroft Island.*

Right: *Cruise ship and kayakers at Blackfish Sound, near Port McNeill.*

*Above: Dawn at Retreat Passage, near
Owl and Midsummer islands.*

*Right: Looking from Vancouver Island
across Georgia Strait towards Texada
Island and the mainland.*

Left: *Dockside at the wharf in Lund.*
Above: *Sea stars and anemones.*

Right: Gulls at Montague Harbour, Galiano Island.

Right: Gulls at Montague Harbour, Galiano Island.

Left: Seine fishing at dawn, Johnstone Strait.

THE
NORTH
COAST

······  ······

Between the northern tip of Vancouver Island and the southernmost point of Alaska lies a lonely coast. Rainwashed and windswept, it is home today to fewer people than it was fifty years ago. The forces of history have touched upon its shores, and passed on.

This north coast was shaped by the same moving glacial ice and debris, rushing meltwaters and eroding wind

······································

Left: Poles at Ninstints, a Haida and United Nations World Heritage Site, in the Queen Charlotte Islands.

Above: Bald eagle in rainforest near Portland Inlet.

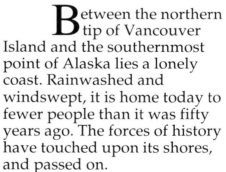

105

Food from the Wild

Salmonberries grow wild all along the coast, from the Queen Charlottes south. Like other berries of the coast, they were important to the native peoples for the variety they gave to a diet ruled by salmon and shellfish. They are one of the earliest berries to ripen on the coast, turning the colour of salmon flesh as early as June. Blackberries, the gardener's scourge, huckleberries, oregon grape and salal berries are other common fruits that grow wild on the coast.

. . . .

Right: Salmonberries and cobweb.

and wave that chiseled the west coast of Vancouver Island. But here, jigsawed into the mainland, lies a broken mass of low islands woven about with sounds, inlets and channels that form a sheltered passageway along the coast. North from latitude 52, the Queen Charlotte Islands raise a long, triangular bulwark against the full heft of the Pacific. Across from the Charlottes, on the mainland coast, a series of deep fjords and river estuaries cuts north and east through the western rim of the Coast Mountains, towards the interior of the province.

Along this coast, the seafloor and the land rise like steps, first gentle, then abrupt. Queen Charlotte Strait, Hecate Strait and Dixon Entrance, the offshore waterways, cover the continental shelf, a shallow undersea lowland that parallels the land. The scattered islands are part of this lowland, tree-clad hills that barely break the surface of the sea. Behind them, serried mountains rise abruptly, their slopes fading blue into the distance.

The waterways that branch inland from Queen Charlotte Sound were first mapped by eighteenth-century British navy men, who named many of them. One named by George Vancouver was Rivers Inlet—so-called not, as might be expected, for rivers that run down to the sea, but for George Pitt, first Baron Rivers of Strathfieldsaye, Hampshire. Coastal historian Captain John Walbran reminds us that Horace Walpole was delighted by Lady Rivers, whom he celebrated in prose as the "lovely wife, all loveliness within and without"; Rivers himself receives short shrift, as "her brutal, half-mad husband."

In years gone by, Rivers Inlet was home to one of the greatest sockeye salmon runs on the coast. The first fish cannery on the inlet opened in 1882; it was followed by a dozen more, on both shores of the inlet. Now, not a single cannery operates on Rivers Inlet; in fact, not one of the eighty canneries that once existed between Vancouver and Prince Rupert is still in operation. The story of their closing is part of the story of the changes that have seen the coast south of Prince Rupert and north of Powell River lose much of its population in the last fifty years.

In the 1920s, there was scarcely an inlet or a protected bay that did not house a handful of settlers, a cannery or a gyppo—a small logging camp, usually set on floats. At almost every one of these settlements, or at a camp nearby, one of the red and black steamers of the Union Steamship line called with mail, with supplies and with news from the outside world. Three classes of passengers sailed aboard the Union boats: men, women and loggers. The loggers were the mainstay, moving from gyppo to gyppo, seeking a few days' or a few weeks' work. The steamships also carried workers for the canneries, at their busiest each summer when the salmon runs reached their height.

The steamships also brought settlers, taking advantage of government offers of homestead land. All up and down the coast, families cleared small patches of land, grew vegetables and tried to pasture livestock, to support themselves and to sell to the loggers and cannery workers.

Technology changed the pattern of the coast. Huge fish packers replaced small fishing boats; fish were taken aboard the refrigerated ships to giant canneries in Vancouver. One by one, the small canneries closed. As the easily accessible timber on the shoreline was cut down, the number of places where gyppos could operate shrank. Forest companies chose instead to bring in heavy equipment and build roads further inland to other stands of timber, and to boom timber down to large mills. The steamship runs grew less frequent, the stops less numerous. By 1960, the last Union Steamship whistle had echoed up an inlet, the last settler's boat put out to sea to meet the steamer at its next port of call. Without

Salmon Spawning

The journey of the Pacific salmon to reproduce itself is an epic story. Early in their maturing year, male and female salmon begin their voyage from far out at sea toward the freshwater stream where they were hatched up to six years earlier. As they enter fresh water, they stop feeding and draw energy from fats and oils stored in their flesh. The males develop humps—large for pink salmon, barely distinguishable for chum—their jaws take on a pronounced hook, and their colour grows deeper or brighter. The colour of the female also changes from its silvery ocean hue to a deeper grey or brown or to bright red. The salmon struggle upstream, fighting the current for days or weeks, until they reach the gravel beds where they hatched. With their tails and bodies, they create nests in the stream bottom, where the females deposit their eggs and the males fertilize them. Male salmon will fight each other fiercely for possession of a spawning female. Once the eggs are deposited and fertilized, the life cycle is complete, the mature salmon die, and eagles and bears come to feast by the riverside.

Right: Spawning chum salmon on northcoast river.

reliable transportation, cannery workers, loggers and settlers all, moved on.

Not that the fish have all left. Rivers Inlet, for example, is famous with sports fishermen the world around, who fly in by float plane to stay at luxurious resorts and fish for record-breaking chinook salmon.

The coast guards its prehistory. There are few known remnants of the first civilizations that were established here, few even of the prehistoric times of the native groups that still live along this coast. Namu is an exception. People have lived at this village on Fitz Hugh Sound for almost 10,000 years, making it one of the longest continually inhabited sites in all of Canada. For more than a decade now, anthropologists have been sifting through the centuries' accumulation of evidence at Namu.

Namu is a continuing story, each layer of the excavation exposing a stage in prehistory. Remains found here—pebble tools, tiny obsidian knife blades, leaf-shaped spearheads, bones and piles of shells—tell us that the earliest residents of Namu ate salmon, seal, sea-lion, dolphin, otter, bear, beaver and dog, creatures that they hunted with their primitive tools. Giant shell middens at Namu display a layered record of life from 5500 years ago to the present time.

Descendants of the ancient people of Namu still live along the coast in small villages such as Bella Bella, home to several people of the Heiltsuk nation, and a once-a-week stopping point for the only coastal ferry that still makes the journey north from Vancouver Island to Prince Rupert. The native culture could survive and thrive along this coast for thousands of years. Not so the culture that replaced it. When harvesting the resources that sustained their communities was no longer profitable, they left the coast. One such abandoned community is Ocean Falls, once a flourishing mill town northeast of Bella Bella. Ocean Falls was founded in the early years of this century to provide a home for logging and mill workers. It was expanded in 1914, when Crown Zellerbach moved in from the United States to start a Canadian operation. The company closed the mill in 1973; the provincial government took over, but even government money could not save the dying town. Today, the Falls is all but abandoned.

Dean and Burke channels, south and east of Ocean Falls, are the "might-have-beens" of coastal history. In 1793, explorer Alexander Mackenzie completed an epic trip across New Caledonia to tidewater at the head of Dean Channel. "Alexander Mackenzie, from Canada, by land, the twenty-second of July, one thousand, seven hundred and ninety-three," he wrote in vermilion and grease upon a rock. His trek is now commemorated by a provincial park on this site. Mackenzie and his men were the first non-natives, guided all the way by natives, to make their way to tidewater along this route; they were not the last. Over the next century, there were several proposals to make this route the pathway for roads and railway lines that would link the coast to the rest of Canada.

Nothing came of the plans; Vancouver and Prince Rupert, not the envisioned city at the head of Dean Channel, benefited from the roads and railways built to link central Canada with the coast. It was only in 1952 that a road—in reality, little more than a cart track—was finally blasted through the Coast Mountains to tidewater.

Its building was a tribute to the can-do spirit of pioneers of the coast and of the Chilcotin, the rolling lake-and-lodgepole-pine ranching country east of the mountains. In 1896, Norwegians from Minnesota arrived at the head of Burke Channel by boat to settle the beautiful valley that pierced the mountains along the Bella Coola River. Many have tried to found utopias on the British Columbia coast; few have

succeeded. The Norwegians persevered, building the town of Hagensborg upriver from the Nuxalk village of Bella Coola, and clearing fields for farming. Until the 1950s, their world was accessible only by boat or float plane, or by a four-day hike across the mountains to the cart tracks of the Chilcotin. Going "outside" was a major adventure.

But the settlers wanted more. Undeterred by repeated government refusals to build a road, they forged their own link east. On a momentous day in 1953, a bulldozer driven by a valley resident touched blades with a Chilcotin cat midway through the mountains on a precipitous slope cut only by the track they had carved from the cliff. Over the years, the road has been improved until today it is paved for almost two-thirds of the way to Williams Lake. Ironically, the building of the road lost the people of the Bella Coola valley their sea route outside. Passenger ferries no longer call at Bella Coola; those who want to travel to or from Bella Coola by sea must summon up a water taxi or private boat.

Bella Bella and Bella Coola are the only major settlements between Powell River and Prince Rupert. Yet the Inside Passage between the two is not deserted. Fishboats head north or south to catch the season opening in each fisheries region; first come the skippers in a hurry, then a flotilla of seiners and trollers travelling in company, then the stragglers rushing to catch the rest. A lone float plane hums past scarcely more than mast high, trapped between the waves and the cloud that presses down on sea and land. All are guided by the flashing beacons of lighthouses that mark the entrances to sea passages so narrow that it is often little more than a stone's throw from boat to bank. Yet the swiftly shelving sea floor allows through to even deep-draught ocean liners. Almost all waterbound traffic use this inside passage, avoiding wherever possible the heavy swells and winds of the less protected route outside the islands.

There is little sign of man's occupation here: just the lighter, brighter green of alder and maple that have grown where cedar and hemlock were cut by loggers from floating gyppos, and tilted pilings that once supported cannery buildings or wharves.

Just north of Princess Royal Inlet, named by Captain Charles Duncan for his ship, Douglas Channel scissors far inland. At the head of the channel live the Kitimaat, "people of the snow," a Haisla-speaking tribe that had dwindled to three hundred by the 1930s, and who now number about one thousand. Since the 1950s, they have been outnumbered by their neighbours, the people of the instant town of Kitimat.

After World War II, the Aluminum Company of Canada sent surveyors to the northwest coast, seeking a site where they could build both a deepwater port whither ships could transport aluminum oxide and a power plant to produce the great quantities of electricity necessary to smelt aluminum. The company built a dam on the Kemano River and diverted the river west through a 16-kilometre tunnel to a giant generating station at Kemano, south of Kitimat. A line carries the power overland to the smelter at Kitimat.

Kitimat lies halfway along one side of a triangle circumscribed almost entirely by water. At the point of the triangle opposite Kitimat is Prince Rupert, at the mouth of the Skeena, the second-largest river entirely within British Columbia. Its nature is best made known by its native name, "water of the clouds." Known, affectionately or otherwise, as the rain capital of Canada, Prince Rupert was created by a railway boom. Though Kaien Island, at the river mouth, has been a meeting place for the Tsimpsean and the Haida peoples for centuries, it attracted few outsiders until 1906, when the Grand Trunk Pacific railway company chose the island as the western terminus for the transcontinental railway line it was building. A land boom ensued, with all the stories of gambling, cheating and being cheated and the making and losing of fortunes that such booms usually entail.

Prince Rupert, they said, was to rival Vancouver; Vancouver barely noticed. The Grand Trunk went broke, and was merged with other railway lines to form Canadian National Railways. Prince Rupert thrived, modestly, as a port and as a centre for fishing, logging and transportation, its history a microcosm of resource use in British Columbia. As logging, fishing, mining and, now, tourism go, so goes Rupert. The city is now an important stopping point on the circle tour, half land, half water, that winds from Vancouver through the interior of the province and back along the coast. Alaska ferries and cruise boats stop here; it's the end of the line for the railway, and the jumping-off point for ferries to Vancouver Island and the Queen Charlottes. It and nearby Port Edward are home to museums showing the life of the North Coast native peoples and the fishery and cannery times now gone by.

Was Metlakatla a sad or a happy story? For nineteenth-century visitors, this colony north of Rupert was a vindication of European civilizing influences, for here in 1859 the lay minister William Duncan established a model village for his Tsimpsean charges. Duncan came from England with a burning desire to convert some natives somewhere, and to show them the benefits of European civilization. Scorned at first, he soldiered on; slowly he made converts. A smallpox epidemic moving with lightning speed up the coast convinced many of the Tsimpsean that their only hope of survival was to leave Fort (now Port) Simpson with Duncan. Together, they built the thirty-five houses and giant octagonal church of Metlakatla, a self-supporting community where every resident worked soberly and industriously. Duncan and the Tsimpsean lived here for twenty-five years; then, fearing the effects of increasing settlement, they moved to New Metlakatla, in Alaska.

North again is the Portland Canal—not a man-made waterway, but a narrow inlet a hundred and fifty kilometres long—and the boundary between Canada and the United States. An accident of history deprived British Columbia of one-third of its natural coastline; Canada is cut off from tidewater for most of the length of the Alaska Panhandle. The Russians, not the British or the Spanish, were the first non-natives to explore and lay claim to this part of the coast. By the mid-1860s, the Russians were weary of their American possessions, and the Americans were at the height of their expansionist fervour. A chance conversation between a Russian statesman and an American businessman revealed that Russia was willing to sell Russian America. In 1867, the United States bought the Russian possessions, including the Alaskan Panhandle, and renamed them Alaska.

The thorny question of the boundary between Canada and Alaska remained to be settled. A commission composed of three Americans, two Canadians and one British member met to settle the question in 1900. The British member sided with the Americans and Canada was cut off from tidewater. Because of their decisions, which engendered great anti-British feeling in Canada, British Columbia's northernmost stretch of coastline is along the Portland Canal.

For thousands of years, some visitors have returned each year to this coastline. Each spring, at the mouths of the Nass, the Skeena and the Kitimat rivers, the silvery, oil-rich oolichans shoal. More highly regarded than gold by the native peoples of the coast, the fish were the major source of oil in the coastal diet, and were carried inland along aptly-named grease trails to be traded with the peoples of the interior. Today, eagles and bears gather near the river mouths early each spring to feast on the oolichans, and humans follow, to scoop up the fish or watch and photograph the animals and birds.

Few Canadians have visited this region, and few know anything about it. Yet one unique watershed which drains into Portland Inlet is rapidly becoming better known here and around the world. In the valley of the Khutzeymateen lives one of Canada's last remaining undisturbed populations of grizzly bears.

Logging has been proposed for the Khutzeymateen, a tidal estuary clothed in ancient Sitka spruce. Though ecological reserve status is under consideration, the question of whether the Khutzeymateen will be set aside as a grizzly bear sanctuary is still unanswered.

Those who wish to log the valley might do well to consider how fleeting man's other attempts to exploit these northern resources have been. In the 1920s and 1930s, 3000 people swelled the region's population, at the copper-smelting town of Anyox on Observatory Inlet. The town closed down in 1935 when copper prices plummeted, the company shipped out every piece of machinery that was worth moving and scavengers scooped up the rest. Fire roared through the valley in 1943, destroying what was left of wooden houses and boardwalks.

Further to the north, at the head of the Portland Canal, Stewart tells a similar, though still-running, story. British Columbia's most northerly port, Stewart peaked in 1910, with a population of 10,000 miners and their families. But resources run out and mineral prices rise and fall. Stewart is down to fewer than 1000 people now, and movie producers seeking mine ruins, glaciers and rugged scenery at times outnumber prospectors. Like other boom-and-bust resource-based towns of British Columbia, Stewart is on its uppers.

The mainland coast ends at Stewart. Across Dixon Entrance and Hecate Strait, the Queen Charlotte Islands are a world apart. The origin of the islands is as shrouded in mystery as the islands themselves are in clouds and mist. Until recently, scientists suggested they were formed by volcanic and other sediments piling up on the ocean floor, or that they were once part of the mainland, thrust 100 kilometres west by upheavals of the earth's crust. More recent evidence suggests they may not have originated on this continent at all, but that they are instead produced by the shifting of tectonic plates from the South Pacific to the north; according to this theory, the islands are the edges of the southern plates, thrown upwards in collision with plates underlying the north Pacific.

Whatever their origins, one thing is certain about the Charlottes: they are unlike any other part of the coast. Recent commentators have tried to dub them the Canadian Galapagos, but no islands could be more unlike Darwin's sun-baked, barren isles of ancient volcanic cones and rock. There is one likeness: the Charlottes, as the Galapagos, are home to species unlike those anywhere else in the world, for here, too, evolutionary forces have been at work on long-isolated islands.

Some scientists suggest that the Charlottes escaped glaciation altogether, others that small pockets called refugia were never iced over. According to the latter theory, the nature of the Charlottes' coast saved the refugia from the glaciers. In the west, the coast plunges steeply, to a sea depth of more than 1000 metres; this is the only place along the Pacific coast of Canada where there is no continental shelf. Instead of collecting in ice sheets along the coast, ice-age snow and ice may have slid down the western slopes of the island into the sea and melted.

If the theory is correct, it explains much about the Charlottes. Here are found species visible nowhere else on the west coast, species found only rarely in the rest of the world that, it is thought, have required at least 10,000 years to evolve. Fossils and pollen found on the islands date back beyond the end of the last ice age along the rest of the coast; did forests grow here while the rest of Canada was smothered in ice?

The species of animals, plants, insects and fish that exist here and nowhere else in the world are part of the islands' uniqueness, as are subspecies that have evolved slightly differently on the Queen Charlottes than they have on the neighbouring mainland. Among these are types of deer mouse, Stellar's jay, black bear and caribou. Some plants have been found only here and in such distant locations as Bhutan and Borneo. An extremely large number of different mosses and liverworts—land plants that resemble green seaweed or leafy mosses—make the islands the moss capital of the world. While not unique, the islands' human history is no less interesting. The Charlottes were and are home to the Haida, the greatest seafarers of the northwest coast. The Haida traveled far up and down the coast in massive cedar canoes, some as long as the ships of the early European explorers. They were warriors, members of the Eagle or the Raven clan, but they were also artists. Their artistic skills and production were at their height when Europeans arrived in the eighteenth century; after an inevitable decline, Haida art has revived in the last three decades.

The totem poles and housefronts they carved are unmatched along the coast. The southernmost Haida village, Ninstints, on Anthony Island, with fallen and standing poles set in a green backdrop of moss and rainforest cedar, has been declared a World Heritage Site by UNESCO.

Those who followed the natives did not treat the forest with the same respect. With the arrival of modern logging machinery, the trees of the Queen Charlottes were harvested with little restraint. Clear-cuts on the mountain slopes brought landslides; landslides devastated streambeds. Until the 1970s, an uneasy tension existed between the loggers on one side and natives and environmentalists on the other. Then, in the mid-1970s, residents who wanted to see at least some of the Charlottes' wilderness preserved banded together and started a fight to save South Moresby Island. They were soon joined by environmentalists in the rest of British Columbia and the world.

It was a long battle. Finally, in 1988, the uniqueness of South Moresby and the Charlottes was recognized, when the federal and provincial governments agreed to set aside South Moresby as a park, to remain unlogged and undeveloped.

That they did so was testimony to the changing attitudes towards the coast. The north coast is a place of unpopulated inlets and moss-draped forests. Most days, it is a landscape of greys, from the slate grey-green-blue of the mountains to the pearl grey of the sky and the mists to the steely grey of the water. Its silent fjords run deep; its steep slopes will never house cities or welcome myriads of tourists to luxury resorts.

Yet westcoasters have said and governments have agreed that some part of this coast that most of us will only glimpse should continue to exist, as it always has, in its ancient and overwhelming beauty and grandeur.

Right: *Houston Stewart Channel, viewed from Kunghit Island, with Rose Inlet ahead.*

The Sea Stars

The Pacific west coast supports more varieties of sea stars than any other region in the world. Sixty-eight species, representing half the world's family of sea stars, are found in the waters off British Columbia. The most common sea stars have five arms, though some have up to twenty-four. The undersurface of each arm is covered with tube feet that can hold the sea star to a surface by suction or move it along at a plodding pace. The ochre sea star is a five-armed creature that preys on mussels and barnacles, and is most often seen in tidal pools or clinging to rocks close to the water. The largest local sea star is the sunflower star, coloured reddish-orange, yellow or purple, with twenty-four arms, and up to a metre wide.

Above: Bat stars and leather stars, with sea lettuce.

Right: Storm waves and Sitka spruce, near Gordon Inlet, South Moresby Island, Queen Charlottes.

Left: *A tour boat boat carries passengers across Fitz Hugh Sound, on the Inside Passage near Namu.*

Above: *Sunset on Calvert Island, site of a proposed provincial park.*

119

Flying the Coast

The day that the first single-engine plane taxied up to the dock of a remote coastal community, the pace of life on the coast changed forever. Now supplies and people could reach any place on the coast in a day, instead of a week or more by sea. Now fishermen, loggers, tourists, residents, could travel almost at will, limited only by their ability to pay and the weather. The advent of float planes gave birth to new legends along the coast: stories of flying blind in fog and cloud and emergency landings in hidden coves, of daring rescues and, sadly, of planes that disappeared forever beneath the surface of the sea. Even the newer planes with their sophisticated technology still draw the same kind of response as they drone overhead: "That's Charlie; he must be going down to Bella Bella for those new engine parts."

Left: Float plane lifts off from Juan Perez Sound, South Moresby Island.
Above: Wave worn rocks at Cape Caution.

Changing Seasons

In winter and spring, torrents fed by abundant rain and then by melting snow rush down the mountainsides into the narrow sea channels of the northern Inside Passage. By late summer, they have dried to almost nothing. The debris and soil washed seaward by the seasonal waterfalls create small deltas at the water's edge, and fish and other marine life come here to feed. These are among the few places on the steep-sided channels where underwater life can thrive.

Left: *Surf Island, near Hakai Passage, north of Bella Bella.*

Above: *Fishing at a pool created by spring runoff in narrow Grenville Channel near Lowe Inlet.*

Following: *Looking across Prince Rupert harbour at Digby Island.*

Sea Lettuce

You can't pick sea lettuce and feast on it as salad, but, dried and cooked, it makes an adequate substitute for spinach. Like other seaweeds, it is a form of algae. It grows normally below the intertidal zone, but occasionally its brilliant green is revealed bunched tightly across the surface of a rock as the tide falls.

Left: Sea lettuce and sea star, at Burnaby Narrows, between Burnaby Island and Dolomite Point.

Above: *Sea lettuce and other seaweeds.*

Right: *Western shore of South Morseby Island, looking towards Louscoone Point and Cape Freeman.*

Above: Dawn on Khutzeymateen Inlet, off Portland Inlet north of Prince Rupert.

Right: Orca and stellar sea lions, Reef Island, Hecate Strait. Shortly after this photograph was taken, the orca grabbed a sea lion from the rocks, dragging it beneath the water to drown. In panic, the other sea lions sought safety in the water and were preyed upon by the entire pod.

Skidegate

By the end of the nineteenth century, the Haida population in the Queen Charlotte Islands had declined dramatically. Reluctantly, the few remaining inhabitants of the small villages moved to Masset at the north end of the islands, or to Skidegate. Skidegate today is the terminus for ferry service from the mainland, and for the water taxi that runs between the two main islands of the Charlottes. Skidegate is the home of skilled craftsmen who carve silver, gold and argillite, a soft black stone found in only a few places.

Left: Bear trails and trees rubbed clean of moss by bears, Khutzeymateen, on the coast north of Prince Rupert.

Above: Skidegate village, Graham Island, Queen Charlottes.

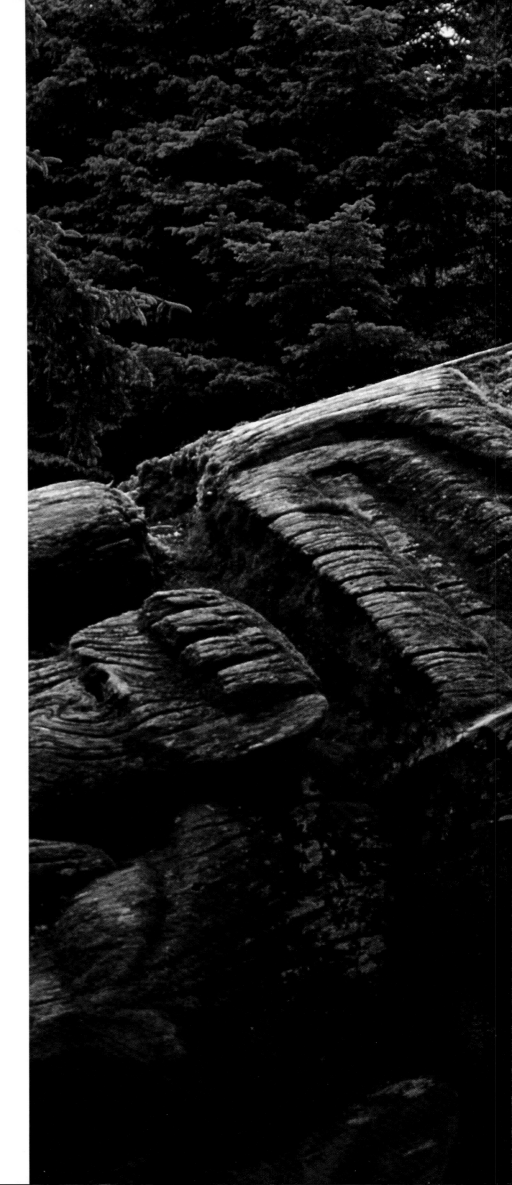

The World of Ninstints

For centuries, the Haida people of the Kunghit tribe lived at Ninstints, on Anthony Island in the Queen Charlottes, protected from outsiders by the strong winds that swirled around their island home. The fierceness of the Kunghit was legendary; when white adventurers arrived on the coast, the Kunghit fought them as aggressively as they had fought any other invader. But they suffered for it: death in battle or by disease resulted from their contact with the white man. By the 1880s, only thirty members of the group remained; by the twentieth century, Ninstints was abandoned to the forest as the survivors moved to Skidegate further north. The heritage of Ninstints remained in its magnificent totems and housefronts. In 1981, Ninstints was recognized as a world heritage site. Now visitors marvel at the twenty-one standing and five fallen totem poles that testify to the strength of this native culture.

. . . .

Above: *Bull kelp near Ninstints, in Louscoone Inlet.*

Right: *Deer and Haida pole, Ninstints, Anthony Island, Queen Charlotte Islands.*

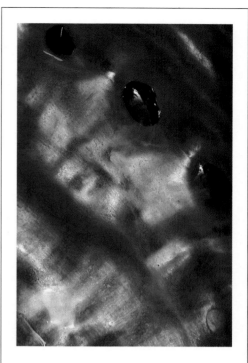

Abalone

Given the mother-of-pearl iridescence of its shell and the succulence of the animal within, it's amazing that any abalone remain on this coast. Indeed, more than one diver has been caught with bags well beyond the legal limit as they strive to meet the demand for abalone in the restaurants of the west coast. Although the mature abalone rarely chooses to move far in its search for the algae that is its diet, it can put on a surprising turn of speed, accompanied by a cloud of mucous that obscures the path behind it when pursued by a creeping sea star. Pacific abalone are the largest in the world. It is the foot that is edible, cut into thin steaks and pounded to break up the tough fibres. Without the pounding, abalone would test the sharpest teeth.

Left: Rose Harbour, South Moresby Island, once the last active whaling station on the coast, now a haven for boaters.

Above: Interior of an abalone shell.

137

The Rainforest

Each creek, each plant, each animal, has its part in the rainforest. The spreading branches of the tallest trees create a canopy, growing fastest and largest in the strongest light. In the shade below, smaller hemlocks and firs grow slowly; when an old tree topples, it is replaced by a younger tree. Mosses festoon the trees and crowd the fallen trunks. Parasitic plants cling to and feed from the hemlocks. Along stream beds, where more light can reach the forest floor, salal and alder compete for space. Fallen trees decay into streams, supplying nutrients for fish and other water creatures. Each element of the forest is interdependent.

Left: Moss-festooned trees in rainforest near Bag Harbour, on the Queen Charlotte Islands.

Above: Murchison Island, off South Moresby in the Queen Charlottes.

The Friendly Lights

Before 1896, the Inside Passage north of Vancouver Island was dark, its hazards unmarked by any friendly light or moaning horn. Then, in the first decades of this century, lighthouses were built all along this coast, to warn mariners of narrow openings to navigable channels, or to mark dangerous rocks or shoals. This lighthouse on Pointers Island, south of Bella Bella, was built in 1907; its white light is visible for thirteen kilometres. The light marks the southern entrance to Lama Passage, a sharp turn to port for vessels heading north to Bella Bella. At first, almost all the lights were manned; for some years now, there has been a fiercely resisted government campaign to replace manned lights with automated beacons.

. . . .

Above: Kumealon Inlet, Grenville Channel.
Right: Pointers Island lighthouse, at the southern entrance to Lama Passage, south of Bella Bella.

The Flying Dolphins

The cry goes up from the ferry deck, "Dolphins on the port side," and camera-carrying tourists rush to photograph the fast-moving mammals. Pacific white-sided dolphins are gregarious creatures, sometimes traveling in herds of up to two thousand. Curious and friendly, they will often follow large and small boats, nosing alongside playfully, then streaking away. They are the aerial acrobats supreme of the west coast; alone among marine mammals, their repertoire includes complete somersaults. Most often, however, they content themselves with a characteristic curved dance into and out of the water.

. . . .

Right: *Pacific white-sided dolphins off Fog Rocks, Fitz Hugh Sound.*

King of the Eagles

It's one of the ironies of life that the bald eagle, the magnificent symbol of the United States, is probably more common along the Canadian coast than in the lower forty-eight states. For years, the bald eagle was a bounty-bird, eagerly sought by hunters because it preyed on sheep and poultry. In the 1960s, it was declared a protected species and has since thrived along the Canadian and Alaskan Pacific coast. It is a highly successful predator, swooping from the top of a coastal snag or from flight high overhead to sink its talons into a fish swimming near the surface, or a seabird it has forced to dive and finally surface, exhausted, for air. The eagle is also a thief, relentlessly chasing other birds of prey such as ospreys until the target bird gives up and drops its prey.

Left: A bald eagle carries his fish catch across Darwin Sound in front of Lyell Island.

Above: Herring fish hooks on commercial fishboat.

Akrigg, G.P.V. and Helen B. *British Columbia Place Names*. Victoria: Sono Nis Press, 1986.

Arima, E.Y. *The West Coast People: The Nootka of Vancouver Island and Cape Flattery*. Victoria: Province of B.C., 1983.

Bodsworth, Fred. *The Pacific Coast*. Toronto: Natural Science of Canada, 1970.

Bryan, Liz. *British Columbia's Coast*. Alaska Geographic, Vol. 13, no. 3 (1986).

Fitzharris, Tim. *The Island: A Natural History of Vancouver Island*. Toronto: Oxford University Press, 1983.

Fladmark, Knut R. *British Columbia Prehistory*. Ottawa: National Museums of Canada, 1986.

Haley, Daphne, ed. *Marine Mammals of Eastern North Pacific and Arctic Waters*. Seattle: Pacific Search Press, 1986.

Horwood, Dennis and Tom Parkin. *Islands for Discovery*. Victoria: Orca, 1989.

Islands Protection Society. *Islands at the Edge*. Vancouver: Douglas and McIntyre, 1984.

Lambert, Philip. *The Sea Stars of British Columbia*. Victoria: British Columbia Provincial Museum Handbook no. 39, 1981.

Lillard, Charles. *Seven Shillings a Year: The History of Vancouver Island*. Ganges, B.C.: Horsdal and Schubart, 1986.

Mozino, Jose Mariano. (Iris Higbie Wilson, ed.) *Noticias de Nutka*. Toronto: McClelland and Stewart, 1970.

Obee, Bruce. *The Pacific Rim Explorer*. Vancouver: Whitecap Books, 1986.

————-. *The Gulf Islands Explorer*. Vancouver: Whitecap Books, 1981.

Raincoast Chronicles. Madeira Park, B.C.: Raincoast Historical Society, 1976-83.

Ricketts, Edward F. et al. *Between Pacific Tides*. Stanford, CA: Stanford University Press, 1985 (fifth edition).

Scott, R. Bruce. *People of the Southwest Coast*. Victoria, 1974.

—-. *Breakers Ahead!* Victoria, 1970.

—-. *Barkley Sound; a History of the Pacific Rim National Park Area*. 1972.

Smith, Ian. *The Unknown Island*. Vancouver: J.J. Douglas, 1973.

Smith, Kathleen M. et al. (ed.) *Nature West Coast*. Vancouver: Discovery Press, 1973.

Spiegel, Ted. Western Shores. *Canada's Pacific Coast*. Toronto: McClelland and Stewart, 1975.

Thomson, Richard E. *Oceanography of the British Columbia Coast*. Ottawa: Department of Fisheries and Oceans, 1981.

Walbran, Captain John T. *British Columbia Coast Names*. Vancouver: J.J. Douglas, 1971.

Watmough, Don. *Pacific Yachting's Cruising Guide to British Columbia: Vol. 4, The West Coast of Vancouver Island*. Vancouver: Whitecap Books, 1984.

Wolferstan, Bill. *Cruising Guide to British Columbia:* Vol. 1, *Gulf Islands and Vancouver Island from Sooke to Courtenay*. Vancouver: Whitecap Books, 1987; Vol. 2, *Desolation Sound and the Discovery Islands*. Vancouver: Whitecap Books, 1989; Vol. 3, *The Sunshine Coast*, Vancouver: Whitecap Books, 1982.

Woodcock, George. *Peoples of the Coast*. Edmonton: Hurtig, 1977.

Young, Cameron et al. *The Forests of British Columbia*. North Vancouver: Whitecap Books, 1985.